NEXT STEPS
in Cross Stitch

NEXT STEPS
in Cross Stitch

ANGELA BEAZLEY

MEREHURST

DEDICATION
This book is dedicated to Eileen and Gordon,
and Doreen and Laurie

THE CHARTS
Some of the designs in this book are very detailed and,
due to inevitable space limitations, the charts may
be shown on a comparatively small scale; in such cases,
readers may find it helpful to have the particular chart
with which they are currently working enlarged.
To ensure the portability of colour charts, they can
either be colour copied, or the coloured areas can be
quickly traced over a black and white photocopied chart
using coloured pencils.

First published in 1996 by Merehurst Limited
Ferry House, 51-57 Lacy Road, Putney,
London SW15 1PR
Copyright © 1996 Merehurst Limited
ISBN 1-85391-529-7

A catalogue record for this book is available
from the British Library.

Edited by Heather Dewhurst
Designed by Janet James
Photography by Polly Wreford
Styling by Nel Lintern
Illustrations by Brihton Illustrations
Charts by Ethan Danielson
Colour separation by Bright Arts
Printed in Singapore by Tien Wah Press

Contents

Introduction 6

What You Will Need 8

Simple Cross Stitch 12
Stargazer Lily Brooch 13
Foxglove Panel 15

Blending Threads 22
Church Window 24
Kingfisher Panel 26

Double Cross Stitch 30
Christmas Tree 32
Herb Garden Cushion 34

Stitching Patterns 40
Oak Leaf Bookmark 41
Tudor House 44

Decorative Beading 55
Pincushion 57
Elephant Cushion 59

Applying Ribbons 64
Winter Window 65
Delphiniums Picture 67

Knots and Loops 76
Small Landscape 77
Garden Gate 80

Semi-sheer Fabrics 89
Waterfall 90
Lily Pond 92

Simple Goldwork 100
Butterfly Picture 101
Sampler 104

Painting and Dyeing 112
Tulip Tray Cloth 113
Cat and Clematis 116

Basic Skills 122

Conversion Chart 125

General Suppliers 127

Index 128

Acknowledgements 128

Introduction

Welcome to *Next Steps in Cross Stitch*. In this book I have combined the skills of counted cross stitch with new and exciting ideas and techniques to enable you to bring a new dimension to your embroidery.

As you work through the chapters of the book, you will learn several new stitches that combine with the adaptable cross stitch, including extended cross stitch, rice stitch and detached chain stitch. Exciting techniques are also introduced to make your projects come to life in a refreshing way. By adding knots and loops, beads and sequins, ribbons or sheer fabric to a cross stitch project, you will see how greater texture can be added to simple cross stitches. Similarly, by adding gold threads and blending filaments, or by using paint and dye, you can increase the dramatic effects.

Each chapter begins by introducing a new stitch or technique to add to your repertoire. Following this, a small project will give you practical experience of your new skill. These quick and easy projects include greetings cards, a pincushion and a brooch. When you are confident of your mastery of the new technique, you can tackle the larger, more complex project which follows. These projects, which include a cushion, pictures and samplers, are designed to stretch and develop your stitching skills. The projects are all illustrated with full-colour photographs and colour-highlighted charts, and accompanied by clear step-by-step instructions for ease of use. To make your work portable, all you have to do is photocopy the chart with which you are currently working, and then trace over any colour-highlighted areas with a coloured pencil.

The designs in this book have been a real treat to develop and stitch. I have used stranded cottons as a base for the projects, and introduced speciality threads for special effects. I have particularly enjoyed using the shiny Marlitt and sparkly Kreinik blending filaments where I wanted to concentrate the eye. Perle cottons have proved useful where dense areas of shiny stitching blend with stranded cottons, while the flower threads and medici wools have given an added naturalistic feel.

I hope you enjoy the stitching surprises that will gradually unfold, and delight yourself, and your family and friends, with your new-found skills.

What You Will Need

MATERIALS

Here are a few tips on using speciality threads. All synthetic threads behave differently from stranded cottons or other natural threads. These points should help avoid any problems.

1. Use short lengths of synthetic thread, about 45 cm (18 in) maximum. This helps to discourage the threads from knotting.

2. When starting and finishing the thread, begin with a knot and then thread the end through at least four or five stitches on the reverse of your work before stitching. End your thread in the same way. Rayon threads in particular have a habit of working free of starting knots.

3. Try to stitch with an even rhythm, and avoid snatching at the thread; this will help to avoid knotting. You can use the thumb of your non-stitching hand to hold the thread close to where it emerges on the front of your work, and let it go as the thread travels back through another hole to complete a stitch. When using several strands in the needle even tension can be more difficult to achieve, especially if the thread has been stranded from different skeins. To keep the threads at the same tension and make sure they lie flat, you can use a trolley needle on the thumb of your non-stitching hand. Trolley needles are useful for laying any speciality threads. As you progress through this book you will learn new techniques and to use new types of thread, many of which would be suitable for use with a trolley needle. Ribbon is an obvious choice (see page 127 for stockists).

The threads used in this book vary in thickness and in their construction. I have tried to give a little variety wherever possible in each design to give different texture to the projects.

STRANDED COTTON

Stranded cotton is the most widely used embroidery thread partly because it can be stranded down into six individual threads, and partly because it comes in such a wide variety of shades. It is often mistakenly referred to as silk, because of the softness of its texture.

PERLE COTTON

Perle cotton is a twisted cotton thread with a shine. It cannot be stranded down and comes in less shades than stranded cotton, but the shades do correspond with those of stranded cotton. It comes in various thicknesses. I have used only Perle No 5 in this book, which gives a good contrast in thickness to stranded cotton.

MARLITT AND RAYON THREADS

Anchor Marlitt is a four-strand rayon thread which can be stranded down. It comes in a good selection of shades and is useful for blending with stranded cotton, or using alone where a shiny finish is wanted.

BLENDING FILAMENTS

There are many of these but the best range of colours I have found is Kreinik. These vary in construction and therefore in thickness but are generally used with another thread (often stranded cotton), hence the term 'blending filament'. They are useful for giving a special effect, and can be fairytale-like when used sparingly.

FLOWER THREADS

These cotton threads cannot be stranded down. As they have no shine, they give a more naturalistic effect than stranded cotton. They have a good range of colours and are very versatile.

CREWEL WOOLS

These fine wools come in many subtle and natural colours. They are used without stranding down and have a nice hairy texture which contrasts well with shiny cottons.

METALLIC THREADS

Threads for goldwork and metallic threads are generally available in shades of gold, silver and bronze. The widest variety of these that are most suitable for counted work are the Madeira range, but many of the Kreinik range can be used in metal thread work too.

RIBBONS

There are many different kinds of ribbon. You will find soft embroidery ribbon very versatile for use with counted cross stitch, while satin ribbons and silk ribbon give a higher lustre but are less flexible when used to stitch through the fabric.

BEADS

There are many different kinds of beads available, although seed beads tend to be much more widely available than embroidery beads, probably because they have a very wide colour selection, and can be purchased with different types of finish on them.

Seed beads are equivalent to one simple cross stitch over Aida fabric, 14 blocks per 2.5 cm (1 in), or evenweave 28 threads per 2.5 cm (1 in). Because of this fact they are very useful for adding a glamorous touch to simple cross stitch. A smaller bead, similar in construction and shape and which corresponds to Aida 18-, or 36-count evenweave can also be bought.

Embroidery beads are small tubular-shaped beads, and bugle beads are longer tubes. Bugle beads are generally identified by their length in millimetres. Oats are beads shaped like an oat seed. There are many others, such as pearl beads, and the names suggest both their character and uses. Sequins are flat mirror-like circles with a hole in the centre. They are generally identified by their diameter in millimetres.

FABRICS

The main qualities required in counted thread fabrics are, that they are evenly woven, and that the dyes are set.

An evenweave is a fabric whose warp thread (vertical on the loom) is the same thickness as its weft thread (horizontal on the loom). Technically this means that Aida blockweave is an evenweave fabric, although the term evenweave is almost certain to refer to a fabric woven of single threads. A possible exception to this rule is Hardanger, which is an evenweave fabric woven in pairs of threads. All this might seem very confusing, so below is a list of the most popular fabrics which are suitable for counted cross stitch.

Aida blockweave

This is a strong cotton fabric characterized by blocks of threads woven evenly into small squares, which are each covered by simple cross stitches. The fabric is very firm and comes in many colours. The most common block sizes are 11 to 2.5 cm (1 in), 14 to 2.5 cm (1 in), 16 to 2.5 cm (1 in), and 18 to 2.5 cm (1 in). Here is a chart showing usage of stranded cotton for each of these, assuming simple cross stitch is to be worked in each case.

Aida block	Number of strands of stranded cotton
11	3
14	2
16	2
18	1

Evenweaves

These are usually cotton, although some new ones exist using threads with a mix of viscose and cotton (for example Brittney). They are woven in the simplest pattern and generally used for simple cross stitch over two threads in each direction. Petit point or half cross stitch is worked over one thread only.

Here is a chart showing some common evenweaves and their various thread counts

Fabric name	Thread count	Stranded cotton coverage
Linda	27	2
Jubilee	28	2
Annabelle	28	2
Brittney	28	2
Lugana	25	2 or 3
Quaker cloth	28	2

There are many more, but this list covers the ones used in this book.

Semi-sheer fabrics

Also used in this book are semi-sheer (or semi-transparent) fabrics. These are chiffon fabrics available from specialist embroidery suppliers. They are available in various colours and are used over a counted thread fabric to give a suble colour change to an area. Twinkle nylon is a semi-sheer fabric with a hint of sparkle. When ordering these, state the size of the piece you require, as they are usually sold in small squares.

TOOLS

In this book we are principally concerned with items that are suitable for working with counted cross stitch. There are a number of aids which make counted work easier.

DAYLIGHT BULBS

In the summer daylight hours are long, and evening work can go on for many hours, but in the winter months daylight hours are short, and the quality of daylight can be poor. For this reason a daylight bulb in your craft or hobby lamp can make matching subtle shades of threads much easier when you need to work by artificial light.

MAGNIFYING EQUIPMENT

Magnifiers come in a range of different types. A simple inexpensive magnifier can be hung round the neck, or magnifying spectacles can be worn. A more sophisticated arrangement is possible where a hobby lamp shines through a magnifier on to your work.

HOOPS AND FRAMES

All counted fabrics look fresher if they are kept flat during working. This is best achieved in a hoop or frame. Here is a brief description of some different kinds of frames and hoops. For instructions on how to use these, see page 122.

Hoops

The simplest and most economical piece of equipment for this purpose is an embroidery hoop. These come in different sizes ranging from 10 cm (4 in) to 30.5 cm (12 in) diameter circles.

Seat frames

A variation of the hoop is the seat frame. It is a wooden hoop on a pole which fits on to a wooden base. The base rests under your thigh, and both hands are free to cross stitch. The hoop part comes in 20 cm (8 in) or 25.5 cm (10 in) sizes.

Slate frames

The slate frame is the simplest form of adjustable frame. It has a few variations, but basically it consists of two short upright bars for the sides into which are slotted roller bars; these make up the upper and lower edges. These have a piece of strong cotton tape attached to them, and should be assembled so that the free edge of the tape faces into the frame. The roller bars can be bought in various lengths. They slot into the upright bars and are secured with small screws at each corner of the frame. Securing the background fabric on to the tape is called dressing the frame and instructions for this are given on page 123.

A deluxe version of the simple slate frame is the floor-standing frame. There are many different types of these, and they vary in price. If you spend hours at your cross stitch you probably need and deserve a good quality one, strong enough to last you through many years of your hobby. The main advantage of these frames is that they leave both hands free to work. Some have a fixed size frame attached, and some have a clamp at the top into which either a

hoop or a slate frame can be fitted. Many floor frames will accommodate a lamp and magnifier attachment.

A number of small accessories are available for use with frames. A chart holder is a useful item which keeps the chart upright in front of you on the floor stand. The chart is secured by magnetic strips. With this, a line magnifier can be placed over the line you are working.

Thread organizers are cards with a series of holes punched along each side. Thread is placed on the holes by a lark's head knot, and withdrawn one strand at a time from the loop of the knot. The shade number and the symbol referring to each colour can be written beside the holes.

MAGNET

Small magnets are useful to keep your needles on when stitching.

TROLLEY NEEDLE

A trolley needle is a large needle with a thumb piece attached. The needle is used to comb thick threads or ribbons so that they lie flat on your work.

SCISSORS

A good pair of scissors is essential. Guard them jealously. A small pair of sharp scissors is best for cross stitch. A separate pair for cutting metallic threads is necessary because the threads will blunt your best pair. A pair of unpicking scissors is useful, and takes some of the pain out of this unpleasant activity by making it quicker and easier.

NEEDLES

There are many different types of needles but for counted cross stitch the tapestry needle is most useful.

Beading straws are very fine sharp needles used for threading beads. Keep them safely in a container of their own, and tidy them away after use as they are very sharp.

Number	Thread	Number of thicknesses
18	tapestry wool	1
20	Perle no 5	1
22	coton a broder 16	1
24	stranded cotton	2
	Medici wool	1
	flower thread	1
	Marlitt	2
26	stranded cotton	1
	Marlitt	1
	blending filament	1 or 2

GRAPH PAPER AND TRACING GRAPH PAPER

These are both useful if you are designing or adapting a design to suit a special occasion. The squares are divided into groups for use with different thread counts.

Simple Cross Stitch

Simple cross stitch is the most basic stitch in the book,
and is the stitch upon which many other counted embroidery stitches
are based. Once you have mastered simple cross stitch,
you can tackle the variations of half cross stitch and quarter stitch,
both of which appear in the projects in this chapter.

In this book you will find many variations of counted cross stitch. The usual cross stitch will therefore be referred to throughout the book as simple cross stitch, to avoid confusion.

Simple cross stitch usually occupies one Aida block or two threads of evenweave in both directions. The only really strict rule to remember with simple cross stitch is that you must always stitch the two diagonals of the simple cross stitch in exactly the same order (usually lower left to upper right, then lower right to upper left) throughout any project. Failure to do this will result in work that looks uneven, because the light falling on your work is interrupted by the different directions of the threads.

Stargazer Lily Brooch

This little design is a simple example of miniature work. The design is stitched over one thread instead of two, which gives it a neat finish at such a scale that at first sight it will not be obvious that the brooch is embroidered at all. This is part of the fascination of miniature work, proving that small *is* beautiful.

This lily brooch is worked in half cross stitch, or tent stitch, which makes it very easy and quick to complete. The brooch setting complements the neatness of the stitched work and makes this brooch a pleasure to stitch and own. One square of the chart represents one thread of the fabric.

YOU WILL NEED

The finished brooch measures 4 cm (1¹/₂ in) in diameter

15 cm (6 in) square of white Quaker cloth
Larger piece of waste fabric
Stranded cottons as listed on the colour key
No 26 tapestry needle
Circular brooch, 4 cm (1¹/₂ in) in diameter (see page 127 for suppliers)

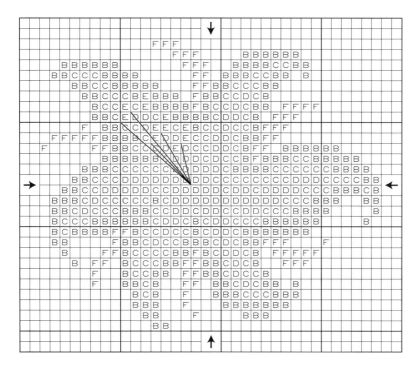

CHART KEY • Stargazer Lily Brooch

Symbol	Colour	Thread	Stitch
B	Pink	Anchor stranded cotton: 25	Half cross stitch
C	Bright pink	Anchor stranded cotton: 26	Half cross stitch
D	Yellow	Anchor stranded cotton: 295	Half cross stitch
E	Golden brown	Anchor stranded cotton: 308	Half cross stitch
F	Green	Anchor stranded cotton: 268	Half cross stitch
	Golden brown	Anchor stranded cotton: 308	Backstitch

STITCHING THE EMBROIDERY

1 To be able to insert the Quaker cloth in a frame or hoop, you need to attach it to a larger piece of fabric first. To do this, machine zigzag the cloth on to a piece of waste fabric of equal weight but large enough to fit your frame or hoop. Turn to the reverse side of the fabric and cut away the waste fabric close to the stitches.
2 Following the chart, work the design in half cross stitch (see page 15), using one strand of the stranded cotton throughout. When the work is complete, remove the waste fabric and press the embroidery gently on the reverse.

MOUNTING THE EMBROIDERY

Place the paper template provided with the brooch on the centre of the embroidery. Carefully draw a pencil line approximately 1 cm (¹/₂ in) larger than the template all the way around the fabric. Machine zigzag just outside the pencil line. Then retrace the stitches with a slightly smaller stitch. Cut away the excess fabric close to the stitches. Baste around the fabric just inside the zigzag stitches. Now place the fabric in the centre of the paper and gather the edges securely. Place this inside the brooch, making sure it is centred (check that the pin is in the right place on the back) and complete the brooch, following the manufacturer's instructions.

Foxglove Panel

The foxglove panel is designed as a celebration of the subtleties and strengths of simple cross stitch. The panel uses many shades of pink in the foxglove flowers, rising from the undergrowth of various shades of green.

Half stitches are used to give detail in the shape of the foxglove buds at the top of the flower spikes. In addition, single strand cross stitch is employed to give the feeling of foliage fading away into the distance.

For greater variety I have used a little Medici wool in the foreground for the tall grasses, and a Kreinik silver blending filament for the wings of the bees.

YOU WILL NEED

The finished embroidery measures
14 cm x 16 cm (5½ in x 6¼ in)

*25 cm x 30 cm (10 in x 12 in) sage green 28-
    count Brittney evenweave fabric*
Nos 20, 24 and 26 tapestry needles
Stranded cottons as listed on the colour key
Silver thread as listed on the colour key
Perle No 5 cottons as listed on the colour key
Medici wools as listed on the colour key
Frame

HALF CROSS STITCH

Half cross stitch is also known as tent stitch and is the stitch most people know from stitching printed canvasses. This is a useful stitch if you want to show an area in the design that is in the distance. It can also be used if you want to introduce a thicker thread which is too thick to use as a simple cross stitch. For example, a Perle no 5 on an Aida block of 14-count would work well using half cross stitch.

HALF STITCHES

Half stitches are not the same as half cross stitches. Half stitches refer to areas of cross stitch where the designer wishes to achieve a diagonal line, not the usual stepped effect and are represented on the charts as shown below.

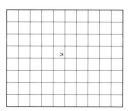

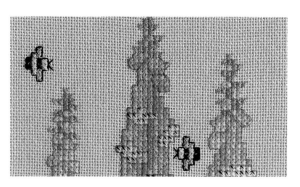

STITCHING THE EMBROIDERY

1 Insert the evenweave fabric in a hoop or frame. Following the colour key and the chart, work all the simple cross stitches. One square of the chart represents two threads of the fabric in each direction. Work all the simple cross stitches with two strands of stranded cotton, except where indicated on the chart key. Work the backstitch with one strand. Use a number 24 needle for two strands of thread and one strand of the wool, a number 26 needle for single stands, and a number 20 needle for the Perle No 5 threads, which should not be stranded down.

2 Work the bees' wings using two strands of silver thread. For a dense effect the bees' wings are worked as two stitches together in the same square. Work a simple cross stitch first, and then a 'plus' shape over this. This is merely a cross turned through 90 degrees. Work the vertical line of the plus then make the horizontal line of the plus. Complete all the bees' wings in this stitch.

3 Now work the backstitch. Outline the bees in black, the central foxglove in maroon, and the other foxgloves in raspberry pink. Work the flecks in the foxgloves in quarter stitches. These travel from the top left-hand corner of the square to the centre and are stitched with one strand of black stranded cotton.

4 Work the stems of the purple flowers using long stitches in one strand of darkest pine green Perle No 5. Work the grasses in the

foreground with straight stitches of one strand of yellowish-green wool. Work the long stitches first, and then use the short stitches to hold the long ones down.

MOUNTING THE EMBROIDERY

Centre your embroidered picture over the backing board, ensuring that the thread lines run parallel with the edges of the board. Lace the back and place in the frame (see page 124).

CHART KEY • Foxglove Panel

Symbol	Colour	Thread	Stitch
◻	Dark sand	DMC stranded cotton: 3045	Simple cross stitch
—	Black	DMC stranded cotton: 310	Simple cross stitch
3	Dark pink	DMC stranded coton: 3688	Simple cross stitch
6	Yellow	DMC stranded cotton: 744	Simple cross stitch
7	Mid pink	DMC stranded cotton: 3354	Simple cross stitch
8	Bright yellow	DMC stranded cotton: 726	Simple cross stitch
9	Pale pink	DMC stranded cotton: 3713	Simple cross stitch
‖	Lavender	DMC stranded cotton: 340	Simple cross stitch
=	Grass green	DMC stranded cotton: 988 (1 str)	Simple cross stitch
∷	Dark blue green Dark grass green	DMC stranded cotton: 501 (1 str) DMC stranded cotton: 987 (1 str)	Simple cross stitch
⊳	Pale grass green	DMC stranded cotton: 989	Simple cross stitch
◇	Darkest pink	DMC stranded cotton: 3687	Simple cross stitch
◹	Silver	Kreinik blending thread: 001C	Small cross and small plus stitch
⊠	Dark grass green Light blue green	DMC stranded cotton: 987 DMC stranded cotton: 502	Simple cross stitch
⊥	Pale grey green	DMC stranded cotton: 3053	Simple cross stitch
⁄⁄	Raspberry pink	DMC stranded cotton: 3350	Simple cross stitch
→	Pale yellow	DMC stranded cotton: 745	Simple cross stitch
⊠	Grass green	DMC stranded cotton: 988 (2 str)	Simple cross stitch
▪▪	Light blue green	DMC stranded cotton: 502 (1 str)	Simple cross stitch
▽	Dark green Dark grass green	DMC stranded cotton: 986 (1 str) DMC stranded cotton: 987 (1 str)	Simple cross stitch
H	Dark pine green	DMC stranded cotton: 319	Simple cross stitch

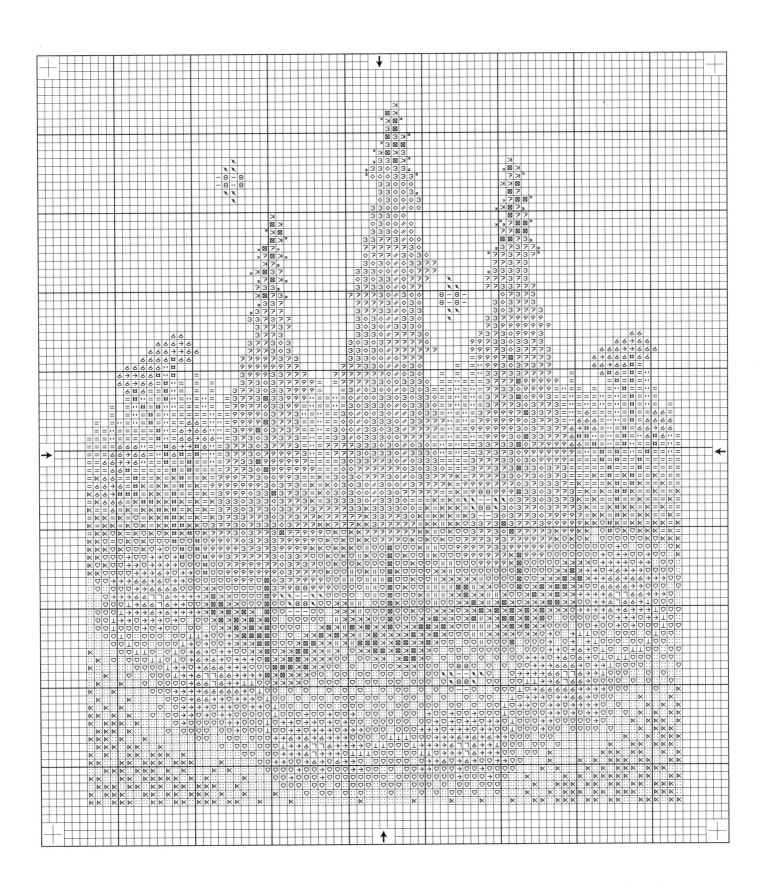

COLOUR CHART KEY • Foxglove Panel

Symbol	Colour	Thread	Stitch
———	Black	DMC stranded cotton: 310 (1 str)	Backstitch
———	Maroon	DMC stranded cotton: 3685 (1 str)	Backstitch
———	Raspberry pink	DMC stranded cotton: 3350 (1 str)	Backstitch
———	Darkest pine green	DMC Perle No 5: 890	Long straight stitch
———	Yellowish-green	Medici wood: 8411	Long straight stitch
———	Black	DMC stranded cotton: 310	Quarter stitch

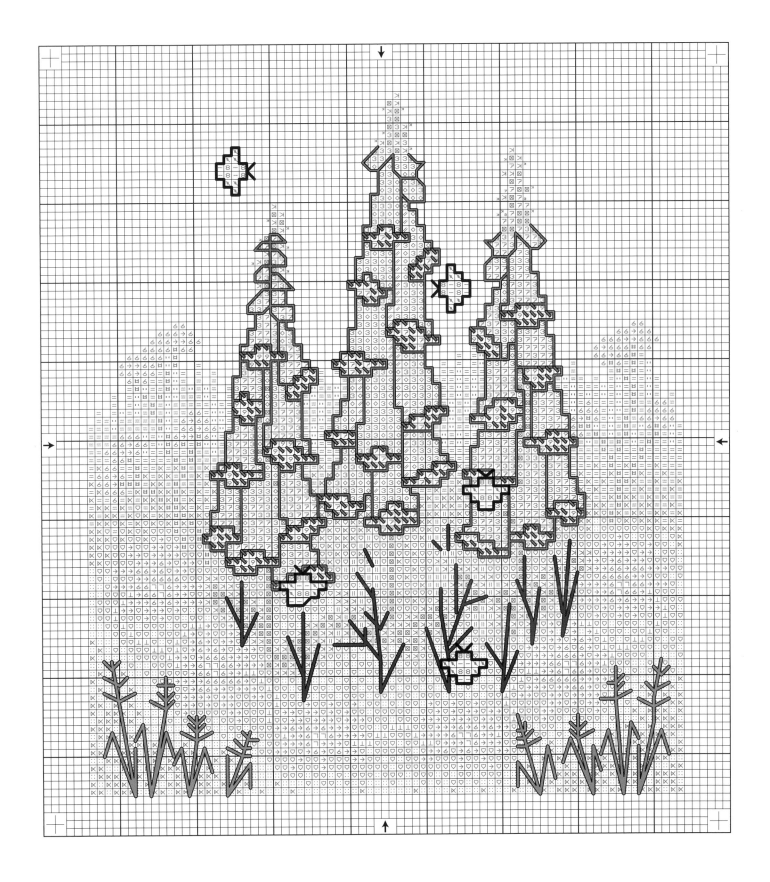

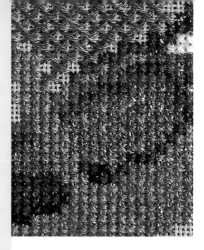

Blending
Threads

Blending two colours together in the needle is a quick way of introducing some dramatic design effects. The uses of this simple technique are explored in this chapter, with both stranded cotton and blending filament. Another variation of simple cross stitch, long cross stitch, is also introduced.

In the previous chapter we saw how using two strands of different shades of stranded cotton could produce new colour effects. Here, the theme is expanded with the introduction of blending filaments and the use of a different stitch, long cross stitch.

The term 'blending' implies that one or more of the threads in the needle is of a different quality to its neighbour. Here I want to show you some of the effects that can be achieved using a range of blending filaments. These fine sparkly threads can be used singly or together with another thread of similar weight (usually

stranded cotton). They can also be used double with stranded cotton or with two different shades of blending filament together in the needle, or any other combination of threads you can think of.

There is one small technical point that is worth noting. The blending filament is made of a fine thread with a sparkly artificial thread wound around it which does not move through the woven threads of your fabric in the same way as pure cotton threads do. It can therefore make it more difficult to achieve an even tension. To help give you perfect tension and

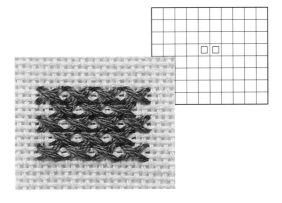

Threading blending filament

Knotting blending thread and stranded cotton

avoid knots and loops on the reverse of your work, try looping the working threads around the eye of the needle in a lark's head knot (see the diagram).

You will note that a double thread is used in the diagram. When using a single blending filament, or one strand of blending filament with a strand of any other thread, take the two threads and loop them in the needle by making a tie (see the diagram).

If an area stitched with one strand of filament is next to another area of two strands of blending filament and a strand of stranded cotton, different textures are introduced to simple cross stitch. This can be a dramatic way of fading a design out around the edges of the stitched area. A fairy-tale effect can also be created in the same way.

LONG CROSS STITCH

Take a look at the illustration of the kingfisher design on page 26 and you will notice a new effect in the foliage of the tree behind the bird. This is worked in long cross stitch.

Long cross stitch is very simple. The technique is exactly the same as for simple cross stitch and the same considerations apply. Make sure that the second thread always lies in the same direction for all your long cross stitches to ensure the work looks even. This stitch looks like a simple cross stitch which has been stretched over two squares of Aida block in one direction, but which still covers one square in the other direction and is represented on the charts as shown below.

Long cross stitch covers more fabric than simple cross stitch and it is quick to do. It also allows more of the fabric to show through. To achieve the same density of coverage as simple cross stitch, you would need to use three strands of stranded cotton for long cross stitch (or three threads of equivalent weight to stranded cotton, depending on the type of thread you are using.)

Of course, it is not always desirable to have this density of coverage. If you have chosen a background fabric of a complementary colour to your design, you will find that two strands of stranded cotton let a little of the fabric colour show through. This can be very effective, especially where a watery look is desired.

Try the smaller project first to practise with these new techniques and threads before going on to stitch the dramatic and densely coloured kingfisher design.

Church Window

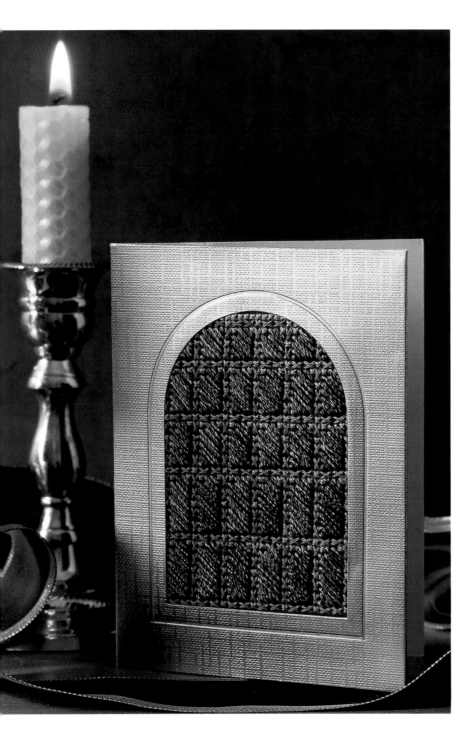

This design is a simple but dramatic depiction of a church window, using rayon thread to suggest the strong colours of stained glass in sunlight. It is a design which could be re-stitched using different colour combinations. One square of the chart represents one square of Aida block.

YOU WILL NEED

The finished card measures 5.5 cm x 8 cm (2¼ in x 3⅛ in)

16 cm (6¼ in) square of navy 14-count Aida fabric
Nos 24 and 26 tapestry needles
Stranded cottons as listed on the colour key
Rayon threads as listed on the colour key
Double-sided tape
118 mm x 91 mm (4½ in x 3½ in) white card with church window aperture (see page 127 for suppliers)

STITCHING THE EMBROIDERY

1 Insert the fabric in a hoop or frame. Two stitches make up the stonework around the stained glass panels. Begin the design by stitching the A symbols first in simple cross stitch and then complete the stonework by stitching the B symbols with long cross stitch. Work the long cross stitch in the same way as simple cross stitch, but taking up two squares of the fabric. The stitches can be worked vertically or horizontally.

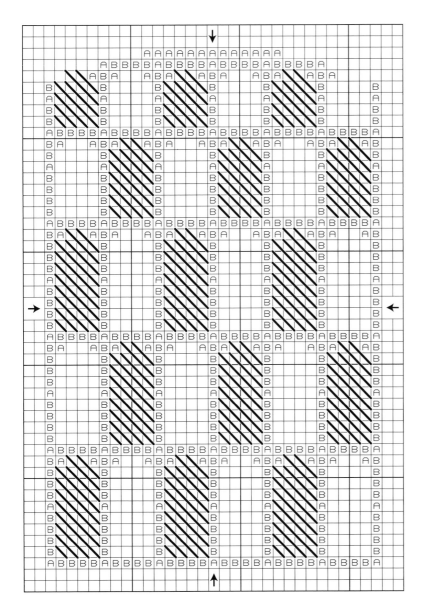

2 When the framework of the design is complete, begin the stained glass window panes. Complete the areas hatched on the chart first. With the three different-coloured strands of rayon thread in the needle, work diagonal stitches in the direction shown on the chart by the hatched lines. Start at the lower left-hand corner of the lower left-hand pane, and work up the arched shape. From the top of this go to the next pane and begin stitching in the same way from the lower left-hand edge. In this way complete the areas hatched on the chart. Finally, fill in the unhatched areas.

MOUNTING THE EMBROIDERY

When you have completed the stitching, press the fabric and trim it carefully to fit just inside the card window. Stick short lengths of double-sided sticky tape on to the right side of the fabric at the corners, close to the edges. Remove the paper covering the tape. With the card open and the right side facing, carefully position the aperture over the stitching. Press down very gently and check that it is in place. If it is, press down more firmly over the sticky tape. If not, carefully remove it and try again. When you are happy with the position of the embroidery, turn the card over and press against the tape from the back as well. Then place four more small pieces of tape over the wrong side of the embroidery near the edges as before. Remove the paper covering the tape and fold the inner flap (on the right of the embroidered area) over the back of your work.

CHART KEY • Church Window

Symbol	Colour	Thread	Stitch
A	Stone	Anchor stranded cotton: 392 (2 str)	Simple cross stitch
B	Dark stone	Anchor stranded cotton: 903 (2 str)	Long cross stitch
\	Bronze	Anchor Marlitt: 1029 (1 str)	Hatched area
	Blue/green	Anchor Marlitt: 1066 (1 str)	Diagonal stitches
	Bright blue	Anchor Marlitt: 836 (1 str)	
	Dark gold	Anchor Marlitt: 1079 (1 str)	Unhatched area
	Bottle green	Anchor Marlitt: 852 (1 str)	Diagonal stitches
	Crimson	Anchor Marlitt: 894 (1 str)	

Kingfisher Panel

This delightful little panel has been designed to recreate the strikingly beautiful depth of colours found in the tiny kingfisher. The strong colours are often mixed with sparkly blending filaments to give a richness usually only glimpsed by the riverbank in summertime.

To contrast with the stunning little bird, the natural shades of the pine tree behind have been worked in long cross stitch. This stitch gives a change of texture, adding to the variety within the picture.

YOU WILL NEED

The finished embroidery measures
12 cm x 14 cm (4¾ in x 5½ in)

*35.5 cm (14 in) square of sage green 28-count
Brittney evenweave fabric
Nos 24 and 26 tapestry needles
Stranded cottons as listed on the colour key
Blending filaments as listed on the colour key
Frame*

STITCHING THE EMBROIDERY

1 Insert the fabric in a hoop or frame. Following the chart and colour key, work the simple cross stitch first. One square of the chart represents two threads of the evenweave fabric. Use the number 24 tapestry needle for stitches involving two or more threads and the number 26 needle for the single strand work. Stitch the bird entirely in simple cross stitch. Work the tree trunk in simple cross stitch using different combinations of colours, and at the lower edge use only one strand to fade out the design.

2 Outline the bird's beak in backstitch using pewter. Work the foliage of the tree in long cross stitch, which is depicted on the chart as a pair of symbols. One pair of symbols is equal to one long cross stitch. The long cross stitches in this design are all worked horizontally. The rows of long cross stitch should all overlap each other by one square.

MOUNTING THE EMBROIDERY

Centre your embroidery picture over the backing board, ensuring that the thread lines run parallel with the edges of the board. Lace the back using strong cotton and place the backing board back into the frame (see page 124).

CHART KEY • Kingfisher Panel

Symbol	Colour	Thread	Stitch
1	White	Anchor stranded cotton: 01 (2 str)	Simple cross stitch
2	Golden sand	Anchor stranded cotton: 368 (2 str)	Simple cross stitch
●	Pale rust Pale rust	Anchor stranded cotton: 369 (1 str) Kreinik blending filaments: K021 (2 str)	Simple cross stitch
4	Rust Copper	Anchor stranded cotton: 349 (1 str) Kreinik blending filaments: K021C (2 str)	Simple cross stitch
5	Chestnut brown	Anchor stranded cotton: 370 (2 str)	Simple cross stitch
6	Dark navy	Anchor stranded cotton: 152 (2 str)	Simple cross stitch
7	Navy blue	Anchor stranded cotton: 164 (2 str)	Simple cross stitch
⎍	Dark turquoise Dark turquoise	Anchor stranded cotton: 170 (1 str) Kreinik blending filaments: K006HL (1 str)	Simple cross stitch
9	Pale turquoise Sky blue	Anchor stranded cotton: 168 (1 str) Kreinik blending filaments: K014HL (1 str)	Simple cross stitch
=	Navy blue Pine green	Anchor stranded cotton: 164 (1 str) Anchor stranded cotton: 879 (1 str)	Simple cross stitch
∴	Pale turquoise	Anchor stranded cotton: 169 (2 str)	Simple cross stitch
⋊	Pine green	Anchor stranded cotton: 879 (2 str)	Simple cross stitch
◇	Turquoise Turquoise	Anchor stranded cotton: 169 (1 str) Kreinik blending filaments: K029 (2 str)	Simple cross stitch
⋈	Dull brown Lichen green	Anchor stranded cotton: 898 (1 str) Anchor stranded cotton: 854 (1 str)	Simple cross stitch
+	Dark grey green Bright green	Anchor stranded cotton: 861 (1 str) Anchor stranded cotton: 268 (1 str)	Long cross stitch
⊥	Light pine green Turquoise	Anchor stranded cotton: 877 (1 str) Kreinik blending filaments: K029 (1 str)	Simple cross stitch
×	Dull brown Pewter	Anchor stranded cotton: 898 (1 str) Anchor stranded cotton: 8581 (1 st)	Simple cross stitch
←	Pewter	Anchor stranded cotton: 8581 (1 str)	Simple cross stitch
△	Grey green	Anchor stranded cotton: 860 (2 str)	Long cross stitch
╱	Dull brown	Anchor stranded cotton: 898 (1 str)	Simple cross stitch
□	Grey green Pale grey green	Anchor stranded cotton: 860 (1 str) Anchor stranded cotton: 859 (1 str)	Long cross stitch
◣	Pewter Dark grey	Anchor stranded cotton: 8581 (1 str) Anchor stranded cotton: 273 (1 str)	Simple cross stitch
C	Black	Anchor stranded cotton: 403 (2 str)	Simple cross stitch
—	Pewter	Anchor stranded cotton: 8581 (1 str)	Backstitch

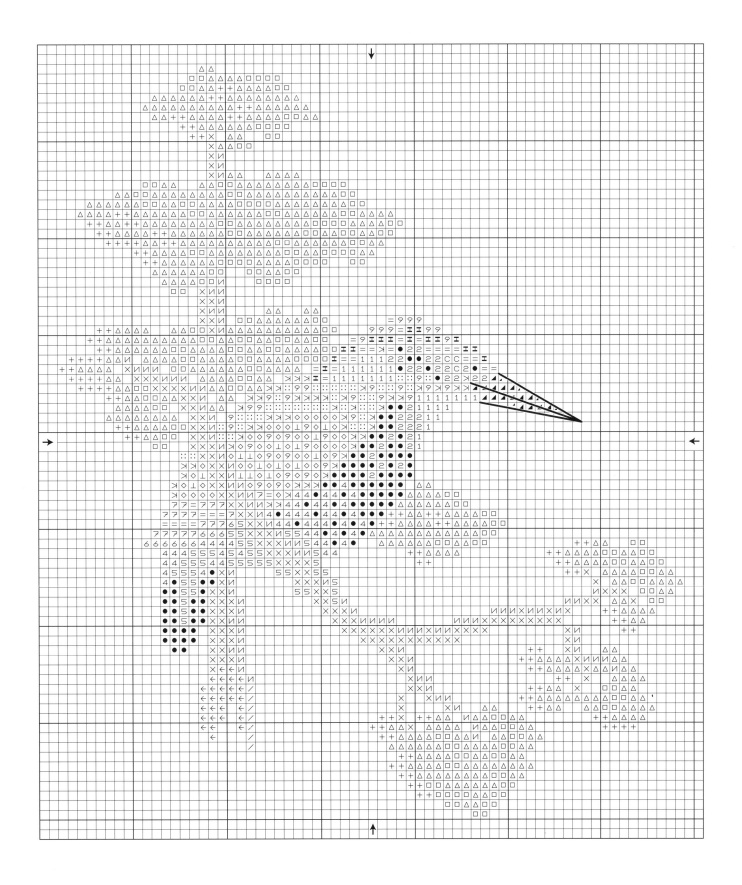

Double Cross Stitch

Double cross stitch is introduced in this chapter. It is a large cross stitch,
covering four times as many squares of a chart as one simple cross stitch.
It can be used to cover an area quickly and it also offers the
chance to blend colours in a new way as each part of the stitch can be
stitched in a different colour.

Inspiration for counted cross stitch often comes from a garden and one of my favourite styles of garden is the formal or Dutch garden. The fascination for me is in the patterns created by the geometric flower beds and the restrained use of colour. Pattern is a strong influence in my designs and pattern making is something that formal garden designers certainly understood, so I have combined these two ideas to make up a cushion design for the main project in this chapter.

Gardens, of course, are much more than just colourful arrangements of pattern. The differences in leaf and petal shapes and textures are as important as their differences in colour. Texture is something that can be achieved by varying the size of the stitches and the thickness of the threads used together in the design.

Double cross stitch is perfect for the needs of this design. It is simple and quick to stitch, covering four times as many squares of your chart as one simple cross stitch. The stitch is made up of two separate stitches placed on top of each other, and in this design each of the two parts of the stitch is stitched in different colours or different shades, enabling you to blend colours in a different way.

This versatile stitch adds a new dimension to counted cross stitch designs. The stitch occupies four times as much space as a single cross stitch which results in two considerations; first you need to use thicker threads to achieve the same colour density as simple cross stitch, and second it covers the fabric very quickly. However, because the thread used is thicker you need to use a fabric with holes that will expand to accommodate the thread comfortably, but you will get a greater texture on the surface of your stitches. All this sounds very complicated, but take heart, it is a very easy stitch.

Double cross stitch, as its name suggests, is made up of two stitches. A large cross stitch, or x stitch, is worked first. On top of this a large plus, or + stitch, is worked. Work the

large cross first in the same way as a simple cross, but ensure that the stitch occupies four threads in each direction. On top of this work the large plus, making the vertical stitch first and then the horizontal stitch. As the second thread always lies in the same direction, this means your work will be even and you will get a smooth finish in the same way as working a simple cross stitch.

Now that the stitch is explained you will be able to see endless possibilities using colours. It is interesting to play with different shades of one colour within the stitch. For example, try the cross stitch in dark green and the plus stitch on top in light green, then try the light green first, and the dark green second. From there you can start experimenting with using different contrasting or complementary colours in the two elements of the stitch to create many exciting effects.

  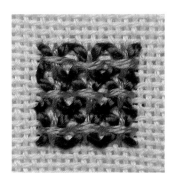

Double cross stitch

Christmas Tree

T o get you started, here is a small design suitable for a Christmas card. This dramatic little design will take a very short time to complete. This design is worked in diagonal rows of double cross stitch to festoon a little fir tree. Look carefully at the chart. You will see the symbols appear in groups of four squares. Each set of four squares represents one double cross stitch.

YOU WILL NEED

The finished card measures 114 mm x 89 mm (4$^{1}/_{2}$ in x 3$^{1}/_{2}$ in)

15 cm (6 in) square of red Linda evenweave fabric
Nos 20, 24 and 26 tapestry needles
Perle No 5 threads as listed on the colour key
Gold thread as listed on the colour key
Blending filament as listed on the colour key
114 mm x 98 mm (4$^{1}/_{2}$ in x 3$^{1}/_{2}$ in) white card with a Christmas tree aperture (see page 126 for suppliers)
Double-sided tape

STITCHING THE EMBROIDERY

Insert the fabric in a hoop or frame. One square of the chart represents two threads of the evenweave fabric. Starting from the centre of the card and fabric, work the double cross stitch in diagonal rows as shown on the chart. Use the number 20 tapestry needle for one strand of Perle No 5 (do not strand this down), the number 24 tapestry needle for one strand of gold thread, and the number 26 needle for two strands of blending filament. If you wish, you can loop the blending filaments over the eye of the needle, as shown on page 23.

MOUNTING THE EMBROIDERY

Follow the instructions given on page 25 to mount the embroidery in the card.

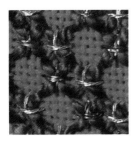

CHART KEY • Christmas Tree

Symbol	Colour	Thread	Stitch
1	Pine green	Anchor Perle No 5: 212 (1 str)	Large cross stitch
	Gold	Kreinik blending filaments: K008 (2 str)	Large plus stitch
2	Emerald green	Anchor Perle No 5: 923 (1 str)	Large cross stitch
	Gold	Anchor Orphir: (1 str)	Large plus stitch

Herb Garden Cushion

I n this stylized cushion design the gardener has tamed nature even in the height of summer. The herb beds are all in full bloom, but not a leaf or petal is out of place. The neat pathways lead to cool fountains and carefully clipped ornamental trees.

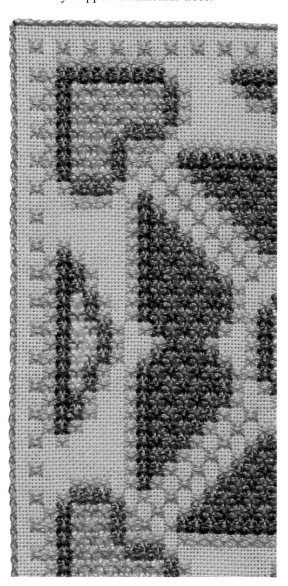

YOU WILL NEED

The finished design measures 22.5 cm (8¾ in) square

50 cm (20 in) square of ecru 27-count Linda evenweave fabric
Nos 20, 24 and 26 tapestry needles
Perle No 5 cotton as listed on the colour key
Stranded cottons as listed on the colour key
50 cm (20 in) square of backing fabric
35 cm (13¾ in) cushion pad
1.5 m (59 in) pink piping cord
Matching sewing thread

STITCHING THE EMBROIDERY

1 Insert the evenweave fabric in a hoop or frame. Each square of the chart represents two threads of the fabric in both directions. Following the colour key and chart, work the garden with its formal layout of herb beds in yellows, pinks and purples. Then work the border with its trees, again formally laid out with a fountain in the centre of each of the four sides. Use the number 20 tapestry needle for a whole strand of Perle No 5 (do not strand this down), the number 24 tapestry needle for two strands of stranded embroidery cotton, and the number 26 needle for just one strand of stranded embroidery cotton.

2 To stitch the beds within the border, begin stitching this design from the centre of the herb bed design. The whole of the herb bed square is stitched in double cross stitch. On the chart one double cross stitch occupies four squares of the chart, arranged in a square.

3 Now work the square line around the beds. A long thread of sand-coloured Perle No 5 is laid between the two threads occupied by one square on the chart. This is placed on to the fabric and couched down with a decorative row of long cross stitches. These are worked in apple green under the trees, and in dark sand under the fountain. At the end of the row take the thread through the fabric on to the back of your work and secure the ends with three or four small stitches behind the laid thread. Snip away the excess thread on the reverse.

Couching a thread

4 Stitch the border using two strands of stranded cotton. Note that the long cross stitches are worked vertically in this design. Stitch the fountains in simple cross stitch with two strands of stranded cotton.

TO MAKE THE CUSHION

Press the embroidery on the reverse side. Centre the embroidered panel, right sides together, on the backing fabric. Baste a line around the design measuring 35 cm (13¾ in) in all directions. Machine along this line on three sides and partially along the fourth edge, leaving enough of an opening to insert the cushion pad. Trim away any excess fabric, leaving a seam 1 cm (⅜ in) from the cut edge. Neaten the raw edges with a machine zigzag stitch or overlocking stitch. Press the seams and turn the cushion cover right side out. Insert a cushion pad and slip stitch the remaining opening, leaving a 2 cm (¾ in) opening for the piping cord. Slip stitch the piping cord in place around the seam. Snip off any excess cord 2 cm (¾ in) from the join, and make a few stitches through the raw ends of the cord to prevent the ends from unravelling. Stitch the ends into the small gap, and close the gap.

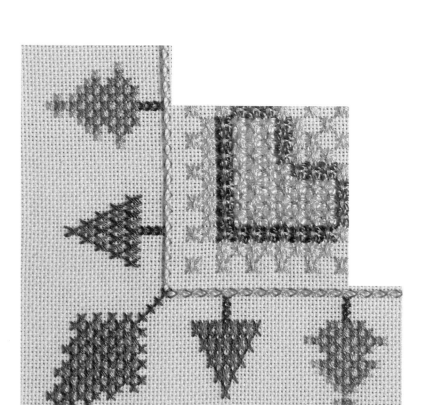

CHART KEY • Herb Bed Square

Symbol	Colour	Thread	Stitch
L	Dark grass green Apple green	Anchor Perle No 5: 267 (1 str) Anchor stranded cotton: 261 (2 str)	Large cross stitch Large plus stitch
5	Dark sand Sand	Anchor stranded cotton: 373 (2 str) Anchor stranded cotton: 372 (2 str)	Large cross stitch Large plus stitch
8	Pale pink Bright pink	Anchor Perle No 5: 23 (1 str) Anchor stranded cotton: 25 (2 str)	Large cross stitch Large plus stitch
◇	Bright pink Light grass green	Anchor Perle No 5: 25 (1 str) Anchor stranded cotton: 265 (2 str)	Large cross stitch Large plus stitch
A	Light pine green Apple green	Anchor Perle No 5: 262 (1 str) Anchor stranded cotton: 261 (2 str)	Large cross stitch Large plus stitch
6	Sand Sand	Anchor stranded cotton: 372 (2 str) Anchor stranded cotton: 372 (1 str)	Large cross stitch Large plus stitch
D	Mauve Bright cerise pink	Anchor Perle No 5: 109 (1 str) Anchor stranded cotton: 98 (2 str)	Large cross stitch Large plus stitch
∧	Light cerise pink Emerald green	Anchor Perle No 5: 96 (1 str) Anchor stranded cotton: 210 (2 str)	Large cross stitch Large plus stitch
＼	Bright yellow Light grass green	Anchor Perle No 5: 295 (1 str) Anchor stranded cotton: 265 (2 str)	Large cross stitch Large plus stitch
C	Pale yellow Bright yellow	Anchor Perle No 5: 292 (1 str) Anchor stranded cotton: 295 (2 str)	Large cross stitch Large plus stitch

Border

Symbol	Colour	Thread	Stitch
E	Sand Apple green	Anchor Perle No 5: 372 (1 str) Anchor stranded cotton: 261 (1 str)	Laid thread Long cross stitch
4	Sand Dark sand	Anchor Perle No 5: 372 (1str) Anchor stranded cotton:373 (1 str)	Laid thread Long cross stitch
+	Light pine green	Anchor stranded cotton: 262 (2 str)	Simple cross stitch
1	Apple green	Anchor stranded cotton: 261 (2 str)	Simple cross stitch
↓	Mid blue	Anchor stranded cotton: 129 (2 str)	Simple cross stitch
2	Mid grass green	Anchor stranded cotton: 266 (2 str)	Simple cross stitch
Ͷ	Light pine green	Anchor stranded cotton: 262 (2 str)	Long cross stitch
←	Dark grass green	Anchor stranded cotton: 267 (2 str)	Long cross stitch
9	White	Anchor stranded cotton: 01 (2 str)	Simple cross stitch
=	Brown	Anchor stranded cotton: 357 (2 str)	Simple cross stitch
7	Pale blue	Anchor stranded cotton: 128 (2 str)	Simple cross stitch
/	Dark sand	Anchor stranded cotton: 373 (2 str)	Simple cross stitch
⊠	Light grass green	Anchor stranded cotton: 265 (2 str)	Simple cross stitch

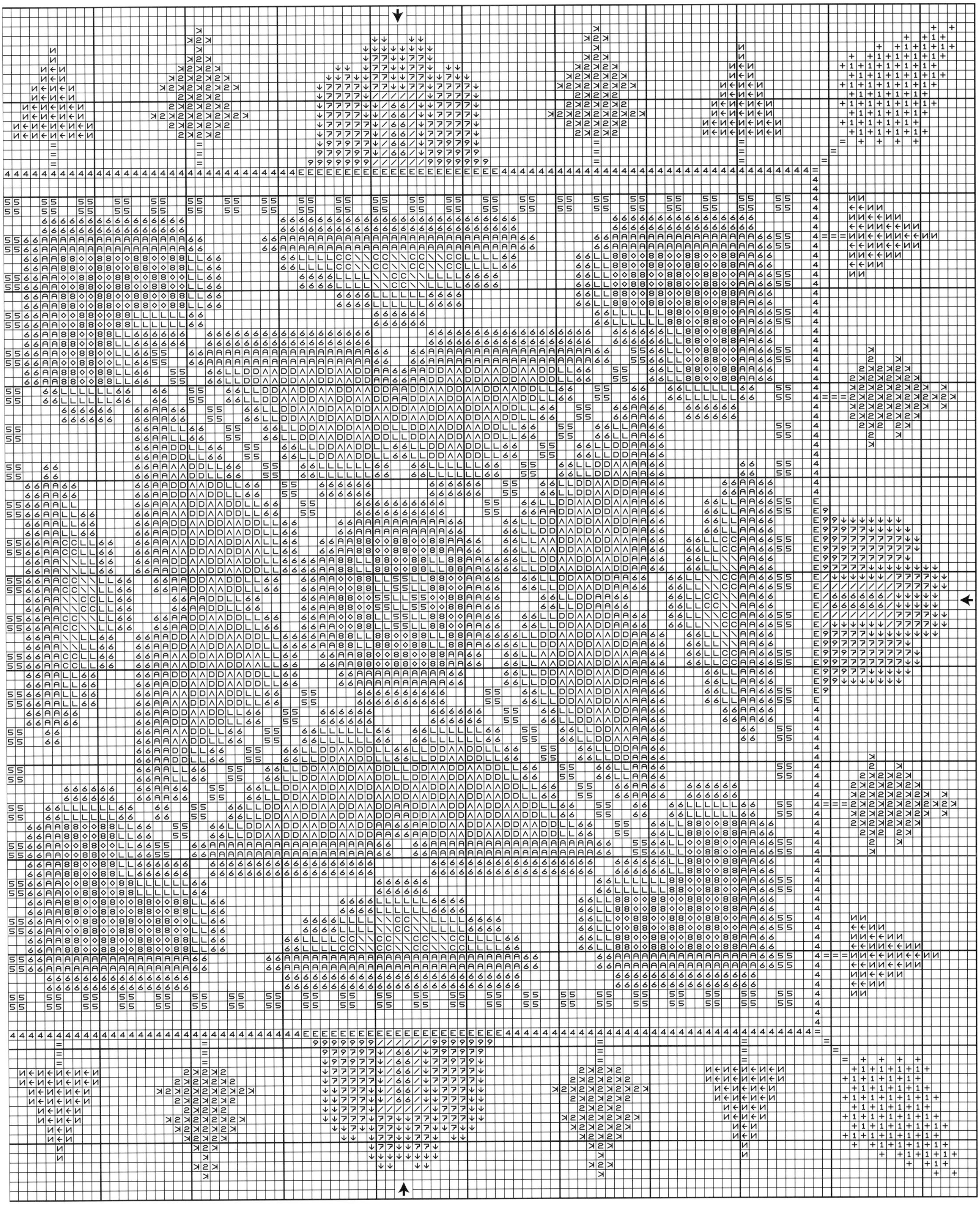

Stitching Patterns

In this chapter we will explore patterns where the fabric is allowed to take a vital part in the design. By expanding the stitches already learned, and adding some new ones, we will build up a collection of different combinations of pattern and colour.

Pattern is a dominant influence in my designs, and geometric patterns are especially suitable for counted embroidery. Simple repeat patterns can be used to create decorative borders for pictures or greetings cards, or they can be featured in their own right, for example in cross stitch samplers. When you combine geometric patterns with different embroidery stitches, you can create an endless source of stitching patterns.

This chapter introduces the technique of stitching patterns with a simply patterned bookmark. Oak leaves provide the basic repeating outlines in the design, and these are filled in with different stitching patterns using a combination of large cross stitches and small plus stitches. Following this, the Tudor House project is a more complex sampler design which is composed of small areas of pattern using a variety of stitches. Most of these stitches have been encountered earlier in the book but a few new stitches are introduced, including eyelet stitch, rice stitch and wheatsheaf stitch.

Oak Leaf Bookmark

This eye-catching design depicts tumbling autumn leaves, just turning from green to brown. When you have worked it, you will see how easily it would be to adapt it to a different leaf shape. Simply trace around a large leaf on to graph paper, and fill with any of the patterns from the Tudor House sampler given in this chapter. You can have fun using many spectacular colours in your stitching. Take a look at the colours on a bright sunny autumn morning. The vivid red leaves of acers and virginia creepers, for example, can inspire you. If you do adapt this design for a brightly coloured leaf, remember that you will get a more naturalistic effect if you shy away from using bright white background fabrics. Why not try a wheat or sage green colour? Either would set off the reds wonderfully.

YOU WILL NEED

The finished bookmark measures 15.5 cm x 5 cm (6⅛ in x 2 in)

12 cm x 20 cm (3¼ in x 3¾ in) 14-count
Yorkshire Aida fabric
Nos 24 and 26 tapestry needles
Stranded cottons as listed on the colour key

STITCHING THE EMBROIDERY

1 Insert the fabric in a hoop or frame. One square of the chart represents one block of Aida fabric. Work the leaf outlines in backstitch using two strands of dark green. Start with the centre of the middle leaf (facing left) and count out to the outline. Use the number 24 needle for two strands of thread and a number 26 needle for single strands.

2 Following the chart for position, fill in the leaves. Make a large cross with two strands of dark grass green. One cross covers four squares of fabric in each direction. Make a small plus with one strand of light golden brown (see the clip detail below). When all the stitches from this step are in place, the large crosses join together to form continuous diagonal lines (see the chart detail on page 43).

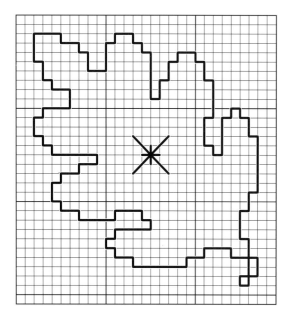

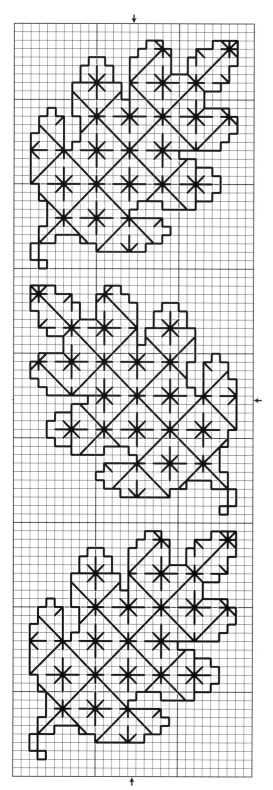

CHART KEY • Oak Leaf Bookmark

Colour	Thread	Stitch
Dark grass green	DMC stranded cotton: 469 (2 str)	Large cross (in backstitch)
Light golden brown	DMC stranded cotton: 782 (1 str)	Small plus (in backstitch) over the large cross
Darker golden brown	DMC stranded cotton: 780 (2 str)	Large plus (in backstitch)
Grass green	DMC stranded cotton: 470 (1 str)	Small cross (in backstitch) over the large plus
Dark green	DMC stranded cotton: 936 (2 str)	Backstitch

3 Make a large plus with two strands of darker golden brown. Make a small cross with one strand of grass green. Complete the outer leaves in the same way, checking the position of the pattern on the chart.

MAKING THE BOOKMARK

Trim four squares from the edge of the stitching all the way around, and fray two squares away on all sides. If you want to cover the back of your work, make a backing the same size as the unfrayed Aida fabric. Stitch a hem in place one square inside the edge. The design would also adapt easily to make a spectacle case.

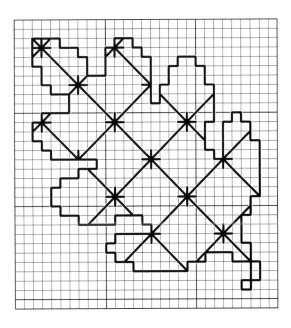

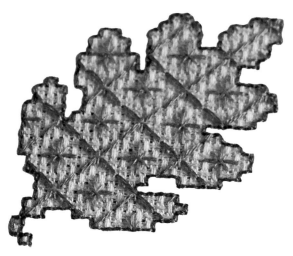

Tudor House

The little geometric shapes of the Tudor house make a perfect design for a sampler. Any geometric stitch can be used, either in a simple form or by introducing a second shade of thread on top of the basic stitch to embellish it.

In this design I have used a matt thread in single thickness for greater texture, and selected only natural shades of stone, brick and foliage. The patterns could also be employed in your own work to complement areas of simple cross stitch.

This design is made entirely from small areas of pattern, each one self-contained in a border of different stitches. Each area will give you a new pattern made up of different combinations of stitches. Some of these stitches will be new, but most have been used in previous chapters. Every thread listed in the key is used singly in the needle.

YOU WILL NEED

The finished embroidery measures
15.5 cm x 12.5 cm (6 in x 5 in)

*35 cm (13¾ in) square of bone 25-count Lugana
    evenweave fabric*
No 26 tapestry needle
Flower threads as listed on the colour key
Frame

STITCHING THE EMBROIDERY

1 On the main chart on page 49 you will see the whole design in outline form. In it one square of the chart represents one thread of the fabric in each direction. Work the outlines first; this will give you a framework to decorate, and it also means you should avoid accidents later. Stitch the vertical beams which run parallel on either side of M1, N1, N2, and M2, and on either side of O1, P1, P2, O2 and so on with brown. The stitch used is a derivative of long cross stitch, worked horizontally but repeated vertically (one stitch under another, in columns).

2 Now begin to work the coded areas, refering to the main chart and the chart details on page 48. If you look at the design, you will see that the areas N1 and N2 are identical, as are M1, M2, J1 and J2, etc. The pattern for these is given once. Stitch the area marked N1 and then repeat it in N2, and so on for areas M1 and M2, etc. Areas N1 and N2 are stitched as follows. Starting at the lower edge of the area, make half of a simple cross stitch using salmon pink. Then make the second half of a simple cross stitch, placing it beside the first, and making sure the two stitches occupy the same hole at the top. Continue making these stitches one after another until you have eight stitches in all. Work another row exactly as the first, on top of the first row. Continue in this way until you have six rows in all. Repeat for area N2. Check that your stitches correspond to the top of the vertical rows of stitching.

3 Using stone thread, work from the lower left-hand edge of area M1 with a large plus stitch over four threads of your fabric in both directions. Work four stitches along the lower edge, and repeat this row twice more, placing each row above the other until the shape of M1 is filled. Then work a small diagonal stitch from the lower left to the top right over two threads, in the centre of each of the large plus stitches.

4 Place a small plus in the centre of the squares left blank using pale gold, over two threads of fabric in each direction. Check the area lines up along the top edge with the vertical rows of brown in N1 and N2, and then repeat for M2.

5 With one strand of gold, work the areas O1 and O2 as follows. From the lower left-hand edge of area O1, count one stitch to the right and bring the needle up. Place a vertical stitch over four threads of the fabric, and make another two stitches in the same way in the next two holes to the right of the first. Come up two holes above the first stitch and make a stitch horizontally that comes down two holes above the third stitch. This is a wheatsheaf stitch. Count two more threads of the fabric and place another wheatsheaf stitch here. Repeat this until you have four wheatsheaf stitches.

6 Work the second row with the same stitches, but place the first at the top right-hand hole of the first. You will need three wheatsheafs for this row. Repeat rows 1 and 2 and then repeat row 1 again. This completes area O1. Repeat for area O2.

7 Work areas P1 and P2. These are only small areas because the window areas E3 and E4 are contained in them. The pattern is more complex; it is made up of three stitches and consists of a long cross stitch worked horizontally, a small plus stitch worked over the long cross stitch, and a simple cross stitch in the gaps left by the first two. Using stone, and starting from the top left-hand corner of area P1, place a long cross stitch over four threads horizontally and two threads vertically. Count four threads to the right and place another long cross stitch in the same way. On the second row count four threads to the right and place another long cross stitch under the gap left by the first two. Continue in this way, leaving a gap under and between each stitch, until the area has been filled, leaving the area occupied by E3 empty. If you find it difficult to do this, backstitch the outline of E3 and E4 in place with dark brown, making backstitches over two threads of the fabric. I find putting simple backstitch outlines on an area first makes later stitching much easier.

8 Using pale gold, make the small plus stitches over the centre of the long cross stitches. Using taupe, make simple cross stitches in the centre of the areas left empty by the earlier stitches, over two threads of the fabric in both directions.

9 Work all E areas in rice stitch. To do this, first make a large cross stitch in dark blue. Then, using pale blue thread, make a diamond shape over this, counting two threads diagonally in each direction. Fill the areas marked E with rice stitches starting from any

Rice stitch

 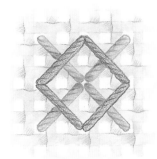 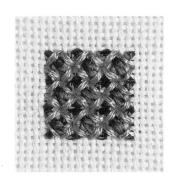

corner. This is a useful stitch which covers the same area as double cross stitches at this scale. It can be used to good effect in your future work.

10 Starting from the top left corner of area Q1, place the second half of a simple cross stitch from top left to lower right, then the first half of a simple cross stitch from top right to lower left. Then make a vertical stitch from the centre of the last two down over two threads. This is called fly stitch. Make one fly stitch and miss four threads, then make another, and miss one. Make the first stitches with salmon pink. Make a further row filling in the gaps left by the first stitches with pale gold. In the second row begin with pale gold and continue making alternate coloured stitches along the row. These two rows form the basic pattern; repeat them until the whole area is complete. Repeat for area Q2.

11 Areas R1 and R2 are made up of long cross stitches, with long cross stitches and small plus stitches over the top. Work from the top left area with gold, placing a long cross stitch alternately along the row. In the gaps left by the first stitches, make a long cross stitch with stone and place a small plus stitch over the top with pale gold. Start with this stitch first on the second row and stitch alternately as before. These two rows make up the pattern. Complete the area and then repeat for R2.

12 Work the eyelet stitches in a clockwise direction. Using brown thread, bring the needle up at the lower left corner and go down two threads diagonally to the left. Keep making stitches this way as indicated on the main chart until you have been all the way around the spokes of the square. You will need to pull the working thread slightly to exaggerate the hole in the centre of the square.

Eyelet stitch

  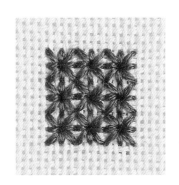

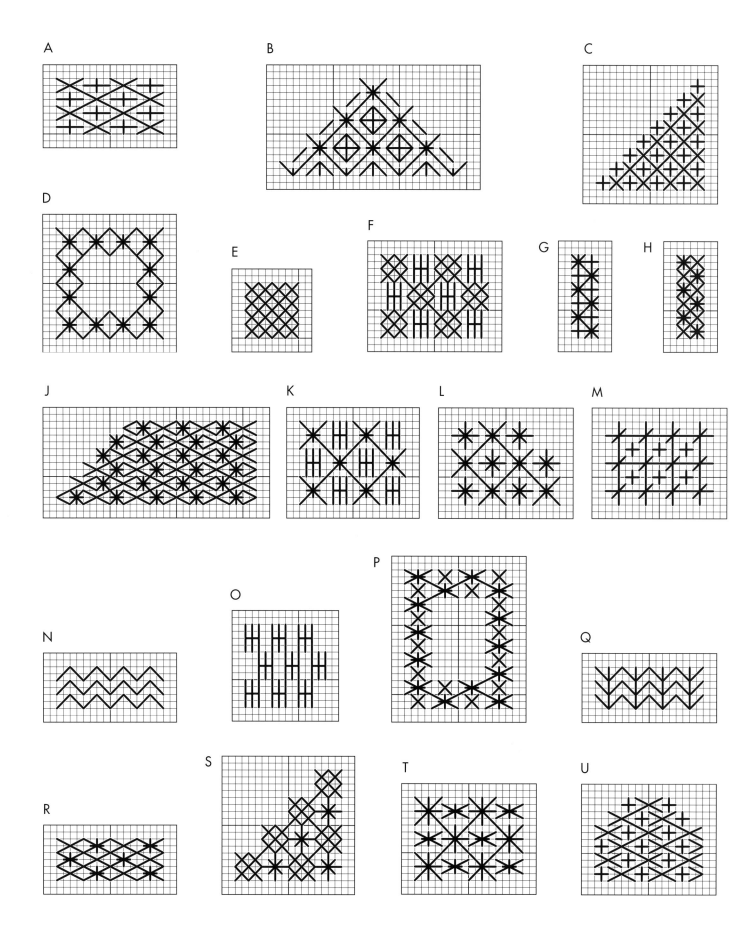

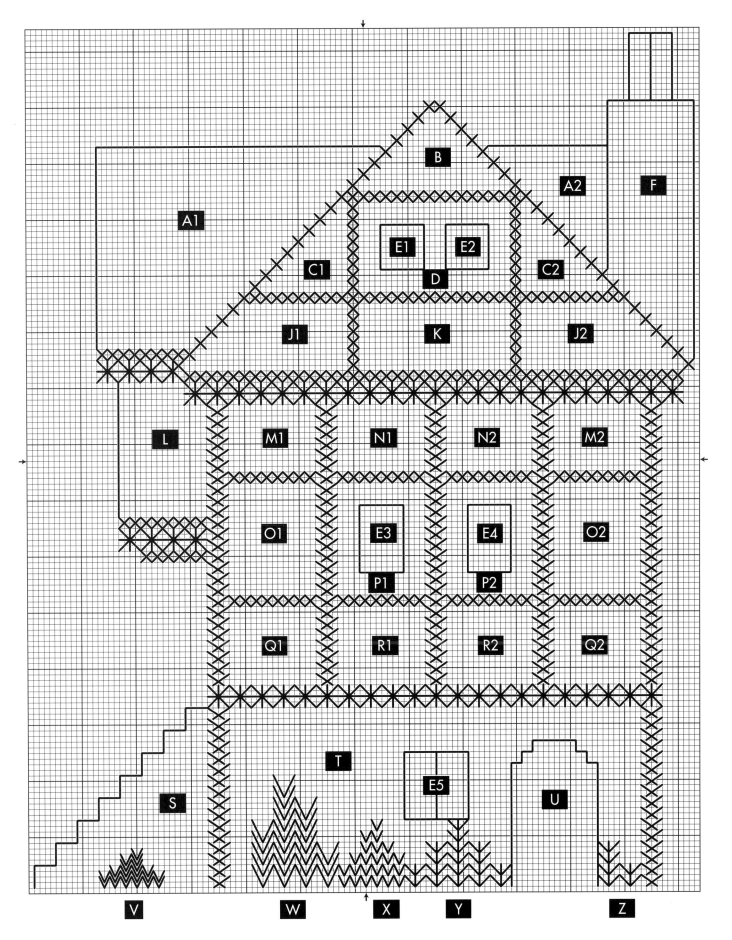

CHART KEY • Tudor House

Area	Colour	Thread	Stitch
Outline	Dark brown	DMC flower thread: 2801 (1 str)	Simple cross stitch
Vertical beams	Brown	DMC flower thread: 2433 (1 str)	Variation on long cross stitch
N1/N2	Salmon pink	DMC flower thread: 2407 (1 str)	Inverted V-shaped stitch
M1/M2	Stone	DMC flower thread: 2642 (1 str)	Large plus stitch and small tent stitch
M1/M2	Pale gold	DMC flower thread: 2738 (1 str)	Small plus stitch
01/02	Gold	DMC flower thread: 2436 (1 str)	Wheatsheaf stitch
P1/P2	Stone	DMC flower thread: 2642 (1 str)	Long cross stitch
P1/P2	Pale gold	DMC flower thread: 2738 (1 str)	Small plus stitch
P1/P2	Taupe	DMC flower thread: 2611 (1 str)	Simple cross stitch
P1/P2	Dark brown	DMC flower thread: 2801 (1 str)	Backstitch
E3/E4	Dark blue	DMC flower thread: 2930 (1 str)	Large cross stitch
E3/E4	Pale blue	DMC flower thread: 2932 (1 str)	Diamond shape stitch
Q1/Q2	Salmon pink	DMC flower thread: 2407 (1 str)	Fly stitch
Q1/Q2	Pale gold	DMC flower thread: 2738 (1 str)	Fly stitch
R1/R2	Gold	DMC flower thread: 2436 (1 str)	Long cross stitch
R1/R2	Stone	DMC flower thread: 2642 (1 str)	Long cross stitch
R1/R2	Pale gold	DMC flower thread: 2738 (1 str)	Small plus stitch
Eyelets	Brown	DMC flower thread: 2433 (1 str)	Eyelet stitch
S	Taupe	DMC flower thread: 2611 (1 str)	Large cross stitch
S	Pale gold	DMC flower thread: 2738 (1 str)	Diamond
S	Pale salmon	DMC flower thread: 2842 (1 str)	Large plus stitch
S	Stone	DMC flower thread: 2642 (1 str)	Simple cross stitch
T	Taupe	DMC flower thread: 2611 (1 str)	Large cross stitch
T	Pale salmon	DMC flower thread: 2842 (1 str)	Large plus stitch
T	Salmon pink	DMC flower thread: 2407 (1 str)	Long cross stitch
T	Pale gold	DMC flower thread: 2738 (1 str)	Small plus stitch
U	Brown	DMC flower thread: 2433 (1 str)	Long cross stitch
U	Dark brown	DMC flower thread: 2801 (1 str)	Small plus stitch
J1/J2	Gold	DMC flower thread: 2436 (1 str)	Long cross stitch
J1/J2	Stone	DMC flower thread: 2642 (1 str)	Simple cross stitch

(continued opposite)

CHART KEY • Tudor House

Area	Colour	Thread	Stitch
J1/J2	Pale salmon	DMC flower thread: 2842 (1 str)	Small plus stitch
K	Pale stone	DMC flower thread: 2643 (1 str)	Large cross stitch and small vertical stitch
K	Stone	DMC flower thread: 2642 (1 str)	Wheatsheaf stitch
C1/C2	Stone	DMC flower thread: 2642 (1 str)	Simple cross stitch
C1/C2	Pale gold	DMC flower thread: 2738 (1 str)	Small plus stitch
D	Taupe	DMC flower thread: 2611 (1 str)	Large cross stitch
D	Salmon pink	DMC flower thread: 2407 (1 str)	Small plus stitch
B	Stone	DMC flower thread: 2642 (1 str)	Large cross stitch
B	Gold	DMC flower thread: 2436 (1 str)	Small plus stitch
B	Pale salmon	DMC flower thread: 2842 (1 str)	Large diamond
B	Grey brown	DMC flower thread: 2640 (1 str)	Large cross inside
A1/A2	Dark brick	DMC flower thread: 2918 (1 str)	Long cross stitch
A1/A2	Brick	DMC flower thread: 2919 (1 str)	Long plus stitch
F	Grey brown	DMC flower thread: 2640 (1 str)	Large diamond
F	Pale salmon	DMC flower thread: 2842 (1 str)	Large cross inside
F	Taupe	DMC flower thread: 2611 (1 str)	Wheatsheaf stitch
G	Dark brick	DMC flower thread: 2918 (1 str)	Small plus stitch
G	Pale gold	DMC flower thread: 2738 (1str)	Simple cross stitch
H	Brick	DMC flower thread: 2919 (1 str)	Simple cross stitch
H	Dark brick	DMC flower thread: 2918 (1 str)	Simple cross stitch
H	Pale salmon	DMC flower thread: 2842 (1 str)	Small plus stitch
V	Dark green	DMC flower thread: 2937 (1 str)	V-shaped stitch
W	Bright green	DMC flower thread: 2469 (1 str)	Enlarged V-shape
Y	Light green	DMC flower thread: 2471 (1 str)	V-shaped stitch with vertical stitch in centre
Z	Dark green	DMC flower thread: 2937 (1 str)	V-shaped stitch with vertical stitch in centre
X	Dark green	DMC flower thread: 2937 (1 str)	V-shaped stitch

13 Outline the steps for area S as for the window outlines. Inside the area outlined, and beginning at the top step, stitch as follows. Using taupe, work the first half of a rice stitch (a large cross) along all the stepped edges. With pale gold make a diamond over the large cross to form a rice stitch. Leave four threads of fabric between each stitch and complete in rows leaving the area occupied by the grasses. In the gaps left, make a large plus stitch with pale salmon, then work a simple cross stitch over the top with stone.

14 In area T, work the outlines of the window and door as before. Fill area T, leaving the space occupied by the bushes at the lower edge blank. Starting at the top left-hand corner, make a large cross with taupe, leaving four threads between each one along the row. Fill the area, alternating stitches in a trellis pattern. Complete the pattern as a double cross stitch using pale salmon pink in a large plus over. Make the pattern that completes the area with salmon pink in a long cross (in the middle of the square), then work a small plus stitch over the top with pale gold.

15 Starting at the lower left corner of area U, the door, make a long cross in brown and repeat two threads apart along the row. Fill the gaps with dark brown, making a small plus stitch. Work the pattern by alternating the stitches, starting the second row with a small plus stitch and repeating rows 1 and 2.

16 The long row of stitches above areas L, M1, M2, N1 and N2 and below area L is made up of eyelets, as is the row under Q1, Q2, R1 and R2. Work all the remaining simple cross

stitches on the main chart and work the remaining backstitch outlines as before.

17 Starting at the top right-hand corner of area J1, work as follows. Using gold, work a long cross stitch and, leaving a gap of two threads, continue in this way along the top row. Using stone, make a simple cross stitch in the gaps, and with pale salmon pink make a small plus stitch over the top. Repeat this pattern, starting with the small double cross stitch under the first long cross, and complete the area making half long cross stitches at the stepped edge as needed. Complete J2 in the same way, starting at the top left-hand corner.

18 Work area K with rows of pale stone large cross stitches with a small vertical stitch in the centre of each. Leaving four threads of the fabric between each stitch, complete the row in this way. Complete the area, starting the second row four threads from the first, and repeating row 1 once. In the gaps left, make a wheatsheaf stitch one thread away from each large cross, with stone.

19 Starting at the lower right-hand edge of C1, and the lower left-hand edge of C2, place a simple cross stitch alternately along the row with stone. With pale gold make a small plus in the gaps. Make row 2 in the same way, starting with the small plus stitch. Continue in this way to fill the areas.

20 Using taupe, make large crosses all around the windows of area D. Using salmon pink, make a small plus stitch over the crosses. Complete the windows as before.

21 Work area B as follows. Starting at the top, make a large cross stitch with stone, and

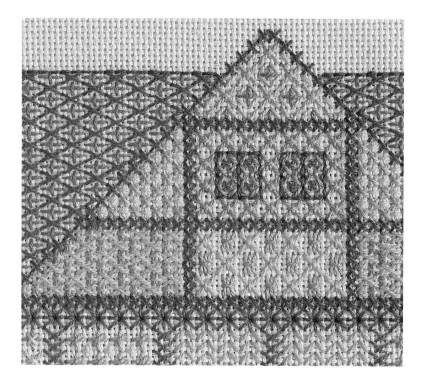

between each stitch. With pale salmon pink make a large cross stitch over the top. Repeat the stitches to form a trellis pattern. Fill in the gaps by making taupe wheatsheaf stitches in the same way as for area K.

24 Starting at the lower edge of area G, work small pluses all over the area with dark brick. Then, starting at the lower right-hand edge, work simple cross stitches over alternate pluses using pale gold.

25 Starting at the lower left-hand corner of area H, work simple cross stitches alternately throughout the area with brick. Fill in the gaps with dark brick simple cross stitches, adding small plus stitches over the top with pale salmon pink.

26 In area V, work a V-shaped stitch over one thread horizontally and two threads vertically in dark green. Using bright green, work an enlarged version of area V over two threads horizontally and four threads vertically in area W. Work area X as for area V, but place the stitches two threads apart vertically.

27 In area Y, work as for areas N1 and N2 but with a vertical stitch in the centre of the V-shape, with light green. Work area Z as for area Y in dark green.

MOUNTING THE EMBROIDERY

Centre your embroidery over the frame's backing board, ensuring that the fabric threads run parallel with the edges of the board. Lace the back of the embroidery and place the board back into the frame (see page 124).

a small plus stitch over the top with gold. Complete the area by repeating this stitch, making a trellis pattern. With pale salmon pink make a large diamond and with grey brown make a large cross in the diamond. Complete the pattern by making part stitches as necessary.

22 Starting from the top left-hand corners of areas A1 and A2, make long cross stitches with dark brick, four threads of the fabric apart, to form a trellis pattern. Using brick, make a long plus stitch in the gaps. Complete the areas with this pattern.

23 Starting at the top left-hand corner of area F, make a large diamond shape with grey brown, leaving four threads of the fabric

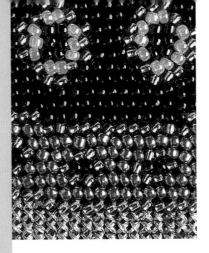

Decorative Beading

Beading is a dramatic technique used to give cross stitch added texture. This chapter explains how to attach beads to your work, how to create loops and tassels, and explores the many different effects open to embroiderers by using beads in a variety of colours and finishes.

Seed beads will fit neatly into either an Aida 14-count fabric, or a 28-count evenweave fabric. Modern manufacturing techniques are such that the beads are a constant size, which ensures an even finish.

Use a beading straw and one strand of stranded cotton in the straw. Knot the end of the cotton, and come up in the middle of the first square you wish to place a bead in. Make two small stitches in the square and then come up at the lower left hole in that square. Your thread is now secured and you are ready to make the first bead stitch. The beads are secured in place by using a diagonal stitch

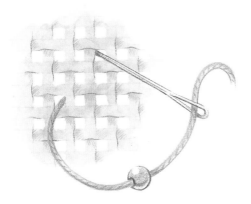

(half cross stitch), working from the lower left to the top right of the Aida fabric.

Work bead stitches in horizontal rows, changing colours or thread and bead as the key instructs. After every four or five beads of one

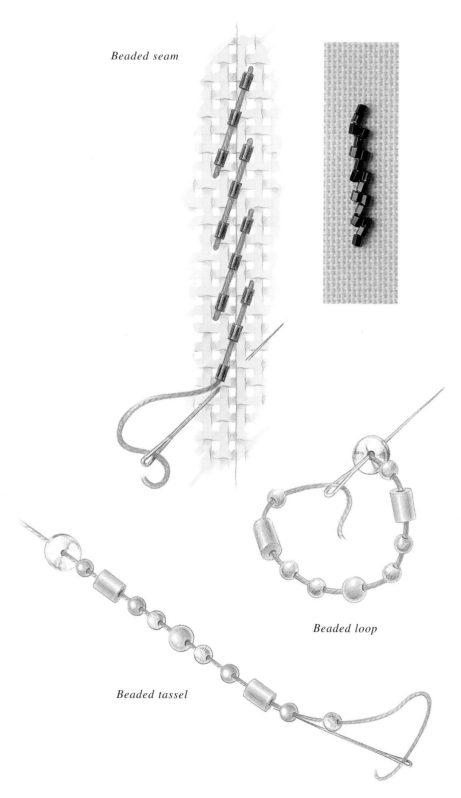

Beaded seam

Beaded loop

Beaded tassel

colour, make another stitch through the bead in the normal way; this helps to secure the stitches and keeps the tension even. If your thread starts to look tired or worn, finish it off at the back of the work by making three small back stitches in the square of Aida occupied by a bead. You can use a knot, too, if desired.

If you find the thread is looking worn very early on in a row of beading, this is an indication that you are pulling the thread too tightly. To compensate for the wear of the thread you can rub it along a piece of beeswax before stitching to strengthen it if you wish. Personally, I find that the stranded cotton recommended in this design is strong and behaves well in the beading straw.

If the thread knots on the front of your fabric, twisting the bead as you work, try guiding the bead with the thumb and forefinger of your free hand until it lies in place on the fabric. This feels strange at first, but after working it for a while you will build up a natural rhythm.

When working areas of beading it is important to keep the tension even. It is easier to work in rows, rather than boxing areas of colour, and then trying to bead the colour in the centre of the ring. For this reason it is easier to have more than one beading needle in use at one time, and keep the spare working threads tidily on the face of your work in a stitch magnet (see page 127), away from the area you are stitching. Beading straws are very sharp; be careful with them when you are not using them. I keep mine in a small tin, one with a close-fitting lid!

Pincushion

Victorian embroiderers often used beads to decorate pincushions. In this design I have imitated some of their ideas. The pale colours of the beads make a stunning effect on black fabric. I have added another dimension to this little design by beading the edges to form a looped border.

YOU WILL NEED

The finished pincushion measures 5 cm (2 in) square

20 cm (8 in) square of black 28-count Linda evenweave fabric
Beading straw
Stranded cotton as listed on the colour key
Seed beads as listed on the colour key (see page 127 for suppliers)
Sewing needle
Black cotton
Small quantity of wadding (or old tights)
Black embroidery beads (see page 127 for suppliers)

STITCHING THE EMBROIDERY

1 Insert the fabric in a hoop or frame. One square of the chart represents two threads of the fabric and one seed bead. Count to the left-hand side of the centre line of the chart and start here. Take the beading straw and thread with one strand of light mauve. Use this throughout for the design in the centre of the cushion. Thread a bead according to the chart and make a small diagonal stitch over two threads of fabric. Thread the next one, following the chart, and make another stitch in the same way. Work in this way, making a long horizontal row of different coloured beads, each stitched with a diagonal stitch.

2 When you have completed three or four stitches, secure the thread and check the tension. Continue beading in rows until the central design is beaded. You will need to bead the little diagonal points as a row on their own after the main design is complete.

MAKING THE PINCUSHION

Make up the pincushion in the same way as a large cushion (see page 36). The finished size of the cushion is 9 cm (3½ in) square. Bead the edges as follows. A 'two steps forward and one step back' edge is the simplest way of describing the beading used here (see illustrations on page 56). With black sewing thread make a couple of small stitches in the seam at the top left corner. Make the beaded edge by threading three black embroidery beads on to the needle, and stitching them down along the seam so that they lie flat, and so that the needle points back one bead's length. Take another three beads on to the needle and stitch these in the same way. Continue all around the edge so that each of the three beads sits in a row but the first of each group sits behind the last. Finish with a few small backstitches to secure the thread. This simple edge can be varied for future use by using different coloured beads.

CHART KEY • Pincushion

Symbol	Colour	Thread	Stitch
A	Light mauve Pale pink	Anchor stranded cotton: 90 (1 str) Seed bead: 186	Diagonal
B	Light mauve Pink and gold	Anchor stranded cotton: 90 (1 str) Seed bead: 124	Diagonal
C	Light mauve Dull gold	Anchor stranded cotton: 90 (1 str) Seed bead: 72	Diagonal
D	Light mauve Turquoise	Anchor stranded cotton: 90 (1 str) Seed bead: 139	Diagonal
E	Light mauve Peacock green	Anchor stranded cotton: 90 (1 str) Seed bead: 148	Diagonal

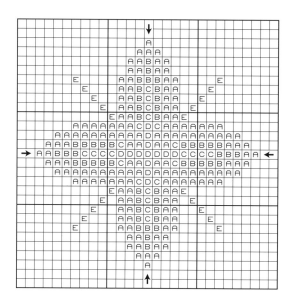

Elephant Cushion

In this cushion I have imitated some of the luxurious qualities of Indian textiles. The design combines seed beads, embroidery beads, bugle beads and ball-shaped beads, together with sequins. To increase your repertoire of techniques I have included loops and tassels in the border of the design. This incorporates beads of different shapes as well as different colours to give your work an extra dimension.

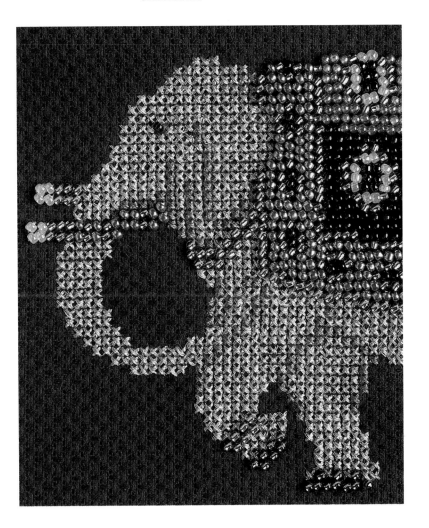

YOU WILL NEED

The finished cushion measures 22 cm x 17 cm (8⅝ in x 6¾ in)

45 cm (18 in) square of navy 14-count Aida fabric
No 26 tapestry needle
Stranded cottons as listed on the colour key
Blending filament as listed on the colour key
Beading straw
Seed beads as listed on the colour key (see page 127 for suppliers)
Speciality beads and sequins (for border) (see page 127 for suppliers)
Tapestry finishing kit, Windsor blue (see page 127 for suppliers)
30.5 cm (12 in) square cushion pad

STITCHING THE EMBROIDERY

1 Insert the fabric in a hoop or frame. One square of the chart represents one Aida block, which is either a simple cross stitch or a seed bead, as listed on the colour key. Following the chart and colour key, work the cross stitch design first, then bead the simple beaded areas.
2 Now work the loops and sequin areas. First work the sequins marked around the border of the dull gold bead. With mid grey in the beading straw, secure the thread behind the area of fabric to be covered by the sequin with small backstitches, and come up through the centre of the circle indicated on the chart. Thread a sequin on to the needle. Secure this by making a loop of beads (see illustration on

page 56). Thread on one green seed bead, one gold bugle bead, one green seed bead, one silver seed bead, one gold bead, one silver seed bead, one green seed bead, one gold bugle bead and finally one green seed bead. Take the needle back down through the centre of the sequin, but do not pull too tightly. Secure the thread at the back of the fabric with three small backstitches. Repeat this process for the six loops along the top and base of the design, and the four loops along the two sides.

3 Create the tassels by threading beads in the same order as given for the loops (see illustration on page 56). Add another silver seed bead on to the thread and push the beads towards the sequin. Holding these in place, bring the thread round the silver end bead, and return the thread through the other beads and down through the centre of the sequin, adjusting the tension as necessary. Secure the thread with a couple of small backstitches as before. Repeat this column of beads twice more in the same sequin. You now have a complete tassel. Work another tassel for the other three corners of the border where the sequin shape is indicated on the chart.

MAKING UP THE CUSHION

When you have completed the embroidery, make the panel up into a cushion following the instructions given in the tapestry finishing kit (see page 127 for suppliers). You will need to decide how far away from the embroidery you wish the velvet to be positioned. I have placed mine close to the beads in the tassels and loops to give a contrast in texture. This makes a rectangular cushion, and means altering the cushion pad by pushing the filling up towards one long side, folding the opposite edge up, and basting in place. For this reason it is best to use a synthetic rather than a feather pad.

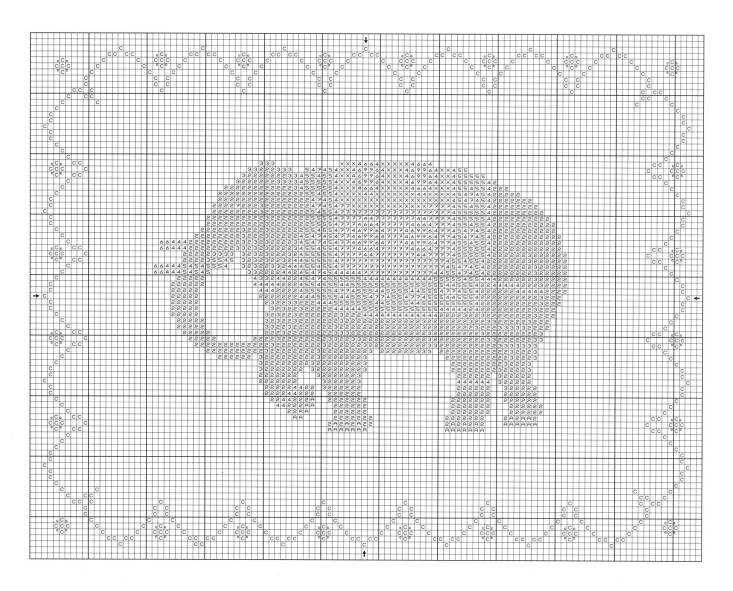

CHART KEY • Elephant Cushion

Symbol	Colour	Thread	Stitch
2	Pale grey Silver	DMC stranded cotton: 648 (1 str) Kreinik blending flament: K001C (2 str)	Simple cross stitch
3	Dark grey	DMC stranded cotton: 646 (2 str)	Simple cross stitch
4	Golden sand Gold	DMC stranded cotton: 729 (1 str) Seed bead: 70	Diagonal stitch
5	Jade green Turquoise	DMC stranded cotton: 964 (1 str) Seed bead: 192	Diagonal stitch
6	White White	DMC stranded cotton: (1 str) Seed bead: 02	Diagonal stitch

(continued opposite)

Symbol	Colour	Thread	Stitch
7	Maroon Deep purple	DMC stranded cotton: 902 (1 str) Seed bead: 13	Diagonal stitch
X	Heather Purple	DMC stranded cotton: 3042 (1 str) Seed bead: 185	Diagonal stitch
9	Dark green Dark blue green	DMC stranded cotton: 934 (1 str) Seed bead: 43	Diagonal stitch
C	Golden sand Dull gold	DMC stranded cotton: 729 (1 str) Seed bead: 72	Diagonal stitch
A	Mid grey Silver	DMC stranded cotton: 646 (1 str) Seed bead: 63	Diagonal stitch

Applying Ribbons

Ribbon has become a popular addition to the embroiderer's workbox
and can be applied very effectively to counted work. In this chapter ribbons
are twisted and folded to add texture, and used as couched thread
to give a silky lustre to a design.

In recent years stitchers all over the world have been making pretty designs with ribbon using free embroidery, but now it is time to see what effects we can achieve using counted ribbon embroidery.

Ribbons have some very persuasive qualities. They have a silky lustre which is bound to enhance any design. They come in various thicknesses, and are therefore going to cover areas very quickly. They can be twisted and folded to give greater textures within a design or used as a couched thread. They can even be stitched into French knots. In fact there is nothing they cannot do, especially now that you can buy embroidery ribbon, which is a very flexible ribbon, ideal for threading through the needle and applying to counted embroidery work.

Winter Window

In this design, the subtler shades of ribbon with their strong sheen are couched down with two different types of cross stitch. This forms a grid through which a simple snowy landscape is viewed.

The window is taller than it is wide so place the longer axis vertically before stitching. The ribbons used are double-faced satin ribbons which have no wrong side. Worked in pale blue, pink and mauve, the colours tie in with the winter theme, but for a more dramatic effect choose ribbons in brighter shades.

YOU WILL NEED

The finished card measures 7 cm x 11 cm (2¾ in x 4½ in)

13 cm x 17 cm (5⅛ in x 6¾ in) pale blue 25-count Lugana evenweave fabric
1.5 mm (⅛ in) double-faced satin ribbons, in three pale colours (see page 127 for suppliers)
Pins
Nos 24 and 26 tapestry needles
Stranded cottons as listed on the colour key
White rayon thread
156 mm x 111 mm (4½ in x 2¾ in) white card with pointed arch aperture (see page 127 for suppliers)

STITCHING THE EMBROIDERY

1 Insert the fabric in a hoop or frame. One square of the chart represents two threads of the fabric. Place a pale blue ribbon vertically along the centre of the design and secure with a pin at both ends. Work large cross stitches over the ribbon with dark salmon pink, following the chart and colour key. Now position the other vertical ribbons and stitch in place using the dark salmon pink.

2 When all vertical ribbons are in place, thread the horizontal ribbons in the gaps between the large cross stitches, where indicated on the chart. When these are in place stitch them down with long cross stitches using the dark salmon pink thread.

3 Complete the design with simple cross stitch as indicated on the chart. Use white rayon thread with two strands where C is marked on the chart. Stitch the area marked B with one strand of white blending filament and one strand of grey green. Stitch the area marked A with two strands of grey green. Outline the top range of hills stitched in white with one strand of rayon thread in backstitch. Outline the other hills with pine green in backstitch, as before.

MAKING UP THE CARDS

Mount the embroidery in the card following the instructions given on page 25.

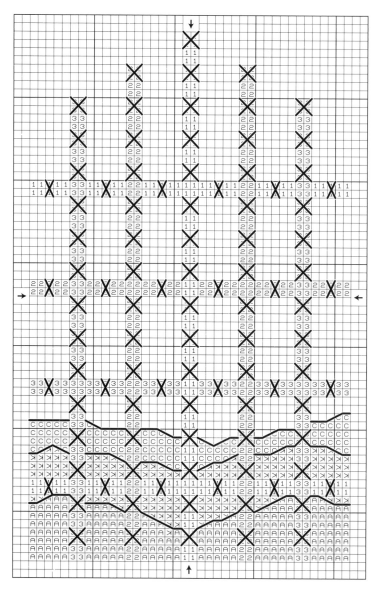

CHART KEY • Winter Window

Symbol	Colour	Thread	Stitch
A	Grey green	Anchor stranded cotton: 859 (2 str)	Simple cross stitch
⊠	Grey green White	Anchor stranded cotton: 859 (1 str) Anchor Marlitt: (1 str)	Simple cross stitch
C	White	Anchor Marlitt: (2 str)	Simple cross stitch
1	Blue Dark salmon pink	Offray satin ribbon: 311 Anchor stranded cotton: 969 (1 str)	Stitched down with large and long cross stitch
2	Pink Dark salmon pink	Offray satin ribbon: 154 Anchor stranded cotton: 969 (1 str)	Stitched down with large and long cross stitch
3	Mauve Dark salmon pink	Offray satin ribbon: 165 Anchor stranded cotton: 969 (1 str)	Stitched down with large and long cross stitch
—	Pine green White	Anchor stranded cotton: 262 (1 str) Anchor Marlitt: (1 str)	Backstitch Backstitch

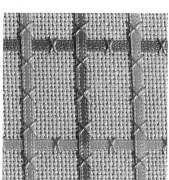

Delphiniums Picture

This is a rich textural design combining many of the techniques already covered in this book. The border incorporates cross stitch, beading and diagonal filling stitches with Perle No 5 to imitate the shine on the ribbons used inside the border. I have used a quick but richly textured ribbon technique to give emphasis to the tall delphinium flowers, and various threads to contrast with the ribbons.

YOU WILL NEED

The finished embroidery measures 16.5 cm x 19.5 cm (6¼ in x 7½ in)

35 cm x 40 cm (13¾ in x 16 in) sage green
  14-count Aida fabric
Nos 20, 24 and 26 tapestry needles
Embroidery ribbons as listed on the colour key
Stranded cottons as listed on the colour key
Beading straw
Seed beads as listed on the colour key
Perle No 5 threads as listed on the colour key
Medici wools as listed on the colour key
Frame

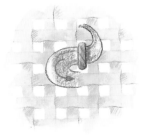

Snake stitch

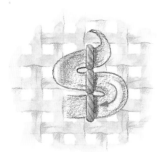

STITCHING THE EMBROIDERY

1 Insert the fabric in a hoop or frame. One square of the chart represents one Aida block. Begin with the trellis behind the delphinium flowers. Thread a long length of 4 mm (⅛ in) emerald ribbon (use a number 20 needle for the thicker ribbon and a number 24 needle for thinner ribbon). Count to the centre of each left-hand area marked K and come up here, work diagonally across the fabric and come down in the centre of the area marked K on the top edge. Once you have one in place it gets easier to place the next threads. From the top, count to the left to the next K section as before and come up here. Travel diagonally down to the point where you take your needle down again and keep making long ribbon stitches in this way until all the K areas are covered.

2 Stitch the J areas in the same way. With one strand of bright green stranded cotton, make a large plus stitch over four blocks of the fabric in each direction where the ribbons cross. Take the ends of ribbon and stitch them down on to the back of the fabric. Three or four stitches will secure the ends. Trim the excess ribbon away. Work the hatched stitches of tent stitch with blue green thread.

3 Work the delphiniums in snake stitch. Start at the top of the left-hand flower spike, thread the embroidery ribbon, and come up in the top left-hand corner of the top symbol D. Make a vertical stitch with one strand of lilac over one square of fabric two squares below where the needle has emerged. Before pulling the thread

tightly in place, thread the ribbon to the left under the stitch.

4 Bring the small needle up again one square below the last stitch and make another small vertical stitch to make a continuous line with the first. Before pulling the thread tightly in place, thread the 4 mm ($\frac{1}{16}$ in) ribbon through it to the right. You will need to adjust the ribbon to keep it occupying the right number of squares according to the chart. Once you start to repeat this, threading the ribbon to left and then right, you will get an even tension beginning to form. The result is a stitch of ribbon which is couched in place, and snakes back and forth all along the length of the delphinium flowers. At the top the spikes are slightly thinner, but once they have widened out to eight squares horizontally they stay at that width. Stop at the lower edge where indicated on the chart and finish the ribbon ends as before for the trellis. Make the other five spikes of delphiniums in the same way.

5 Decorate the spikes with beads in the centres as indicated on the chart. Thread a beading straw with one strand of stranded cotton as indicated on the bead key and stitch the beads in the same way as given on pages 55-56. Complete the rest of the picture area inside the border according to the information given in the detailed notes on the colour key.

6 Work the small yellow flowers using the 2 mm ($\frac{1}{16}$ in) ribbon as an embroidery thread and sew up from the outside of the petals,

always going down into the middle of the flower. Work around the flower shape in a clockwise direction, starting from the lower left petal.

7 Work the long grasses around the little yellow flowers with long straight stitches of dark emerald green Perle No 5. Work the long stems of the delphiniums with two strands of Medici wool in dull green, and catch down the stems occasionally with the little vertical stitches as shown on the chart.

8 Work the border in rows from the inside. Follow the detailed instructions as before. See the border chart on page 72 for the direction of the stitches. The Perle shade of light pine green always travels in this direction \, and the shade of bright green always travels in this direction /. The Perle squares are best worked in the same way as satin stitch, always starting the next stitch underneath the first, the thread travelling in the same direction each time. Start with the smallest stitch and work towards the longest, and then work towards the smallest again. Attach the beads where indicated in the same way as before.

MOUNTING THE EMBROIDERY

Centre your embroidery over the frame's backing board, ensuring that the fabric threads run parallel with the edges of the board. Lace the back of the embroidery and place the board back into the frame (see page 124).

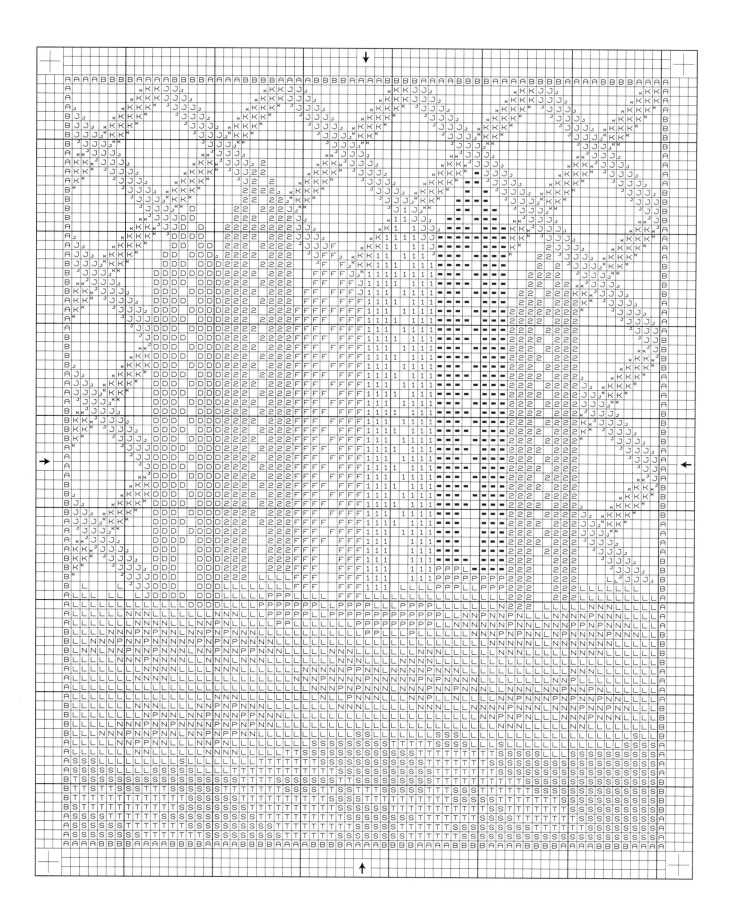

CHART KEY • Delphiniums Picture

Trellis

Symbol	Colour	Thread	Stitch
J	Moss	Offray ribbon: 570 [4mm (1/8 in)]	
K	Emerald	Offray ribbon: 580 [4mm (1/8 in)]	
	Bright green	Anchor stranded cotton: 268 (1 str)	Large plus stitch
Trellis hatched lines			
	Blue green	Anchor stranded cotton: 878 (1 str)	Tent stitch

Delphiniums

Symbol	Colour	Thread	Stitch
D	Lilac	Anchor stranded cotton: 117 (1 str)	Small vertical stitches to hold ribbon
	Blue vapour	Offray ribbon: 303 [4mm (1/8 in)]	Snake stitch
2	Lilac	Anchor stranded cotton: 117 (1 str)	Small vertical stitches to hold ribbon
	Grape	Offray ribbon: 463 [4mm (1/8 in)]	Snake stitch
F	Lilac	Anchor stranded cotton: 117 (1 str)	Small vertical stitches to hold ribbon
	French blue	Offray ribbon: 332 [4mm (1/8 in)]	Snake stitch
1	Pale grape	Anchor stranded cotton: 871 (1 str)	Small vertical stitches to hold ribbon
	Thistle	Offray ribbon: 435 [4mm (1/8 in)]	Snake stitch
▬	Pink	Anchor stranded cotton: 90 (1 str)	Small vertical stitches to hold ribbon
	Orchid	Offray ribbon: 430 [4mm (1/8 in)]	Snake stitch

(continued on page 72)

CHART KEY • Delphiniums Picture *(continued)*

Border

Symbol	Colour	Thread	Stitch
A	Bright green	Anchor stranded cotton: 268 (2 str)	Simple cross stitch
C	Dark pine green	Anchor stranded cotton: 862 (2 str)	Simple cross stitch
B	Bright green Green and purple	Anchor stranded cotton: 268 (1 str) Bead: 142	Diagonal stitch
Border hatched lines	Bright green	Anchor Perle No 5: 268 (1 str)	Tent stitch blocks (in this direction /)
Border hatched lines	Light pine green	Anchor Perle No 5: 263 (1 str)	Tent stitch blocks (in this direction \)

Foreground

Symbol	Colour	Thread	Stitch
N	Dull green	Medici wool: 8412 (1 str)	Simple cross stitch
P	Dark grass green	Medici wool: 8402 (1 str)	Simple cross stitch
S	Blue green	Medici wool: 8406 (2 str)	Tent stitch
T	Grass green	Medici wood: 8346 (2 str)	Tent stitch
L	Light pine green	Anchor Perle No 5: 263 (1 str)	Tent stitch

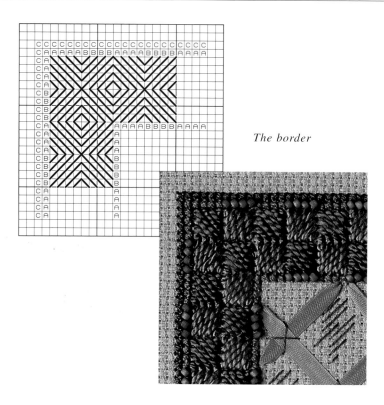

The border

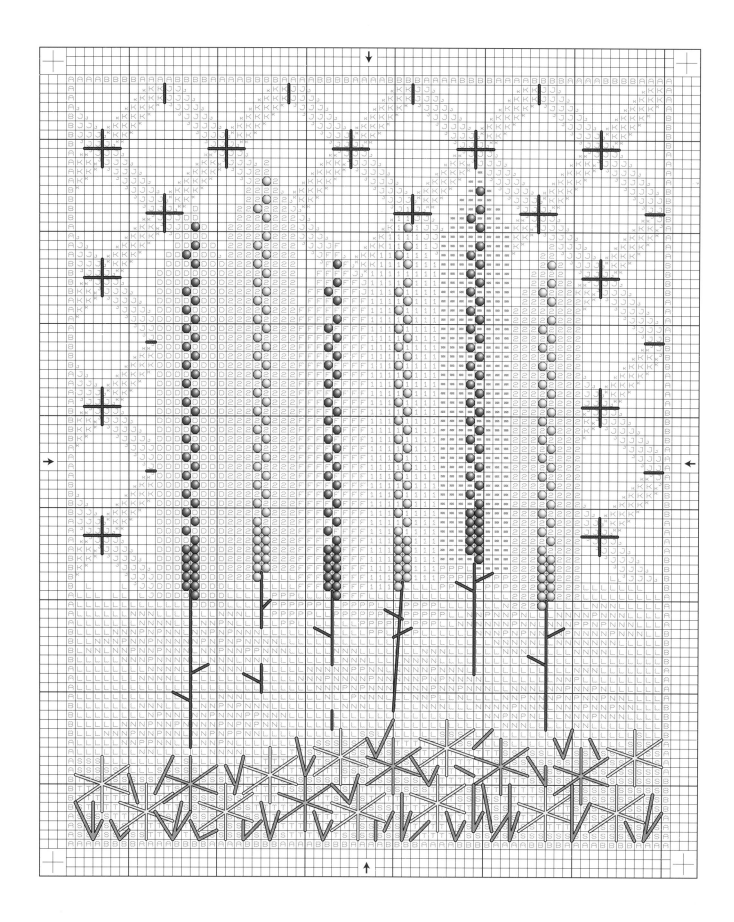

COLOUR CHART KEY • Delphiniums Picture

Foreground

Symbol	Colour	Thread	Stitch
◉	Light purple Pale blue	Anchor stranded cotton: 108 (1 str) Bead: 147	Diagonal stitch on delphinium
◎	Light purple Frosted purple	Anchor stranded cotton: 108 (1 str) Bead: 141	Diagonal stitch on delphinium
▬	Dull green	Medici wool: 8412 (2 str)	Straight stitch
▬	Bright green	Anchor stranded cotton: 268 (1 str)	Large plus stitch to hold ribbon
═	Daffodil	Offray ribbon: 645 [2mm (¹⁄₁₆ in)]	Long stitch
═	Yellow gold	Offray ribbon: 660 [2mm (¹⁄₁₆ in)]	Long stitch
▬	Dark emerald green	Anchor Perle No 5: 212 (1 str)	Long stitch

Knots and Loops

*Knots and loops can be used in cross stitch embroidery to soften shapes
and add texture to a design. This chapter introduces french knots
and demonstrates how you can vary their size to produce remarkably
different effects.*

Some of the most interesting free embroidery
effects translate well into counted work. The
techniques of knotted and looped stitches can
offer a natural element to an otherwise more
formal finished project. If you want to soften
shapes and lift areas to give a raised or
textured finish, simple knots and loops are
perfect. French knots are the best loved 'little
flower' stitches. This very simple knotting
technique can be varied to give different-sized
knots, created by using different thicknesses
of embroidery threads, and by wrapping the
thread around the needle more times: once for
a tiny bud, twice for a little flower, and three
times for a full-blown bloom.

In the smaller design you will see how
french knots can transform a simple design
into a really colourful mini project. This is also
a good time to learn how to avoid the scourge
of all embroiderers: disappearing French knots.
I often hear of this great plague sweeping the
nation; although it is distressing, it can be very
easily avoided. There are two simple rules to
follow. First, never come up and down through
the same hole in the fabric, or if you do make
sure you take the needle around a stitched
thread lying over that hole. Second, do not pull
the knot tightly. Experiment with tension, and
find the perfect knot size by varying the
amount you pull the thread from the back.

Small Landscape

Fields of corn with eye-catching poppies nodding in the breeze make the simplest of stitches dramatic. When you have mastered the technique of layering long vertical stitches in rows coming down the design, you could use it to represent any small countryside scene. Simply change the colour of the knots in the foreground to suggest other flowers.

YOU WILL NEED

The finished design measures 8 cm (3⅛ in) in diameter

15 cm (6 in) square of pale blue 28-count
Annabelle evenweave fabric
Nos 22, 24 and 26 tapestry needles
Flower threads as listed on the colour key
Circular frame with an 8 cm (3⅛ in) aperture
(see page 127 for suppliers)
Basting thread

STITCHING THE EMBROIDERY

1 Draw around the card shape on to the fabric, and baste this shape. This is your design area. Insert the fabric into a hoop or frame. This design is worked mainly in long straight stitches. The chart shows the first row, starting from the top of the stitched area of the design. One square of the chart represents two threads of the fabric in each direction. Begin stitching so that the first row lies halfway up the fabric. Subsequent rows are repeats of this one, starting eight threads below the first. The colour sequence varies on each row.

2 Work the top row using two threads of sand where you see the long straight stitches. In between these work the second row of long straight stitches with two threads of stone. Form long straight stitches, working from the lower left knot to the upper left knot, and so on along the row. Place a second row under the first row as follows: eight threads beneath the sand stitches on the top row, work in the same

way with two threads of blue green. Under the corn-coloured stitches on the top row is grass green. Now work the third row using two threads of avocado green under the blue green, and dark emerald green under the grass green. Finish the bare patches with long straight stitches of blue green.

3 Work the poppies with french knots at random, using two threads of dark red. Wrap the thread round the needle once for the first stitch, twice for the second, and three times for the third. In between these place poppies with light red.

Making a french knot

4 To work the corn heads (see the photograph), place four or five long diagonal stitches of one strand of corn from the lower edge of the first row to six or eight threads above the first row. Around the tops of the stitches work small french knots, winding the thread around the needle once only following the diagram (see above). Place some poppy stems under the flower heads at random using two threads of blue green.

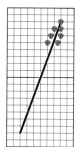

A head of corn

MOUNTING THE EMBROIDERY

Cut the fabric 2 cm (¾ in) larger than the circular aperture of the frame all the way around. Baste with 1cm (½ in) long stitches, 1cm (½ in) in from the raw edge. Pull up the basting thread at both ends to encase the paper circle supplied with the frame. When the fabric is secured inside the gathered edges knot the basting thread ends. Place the embroidery behind the glass, and into the frame, making sure the backing is placed in with the hanger at the right angle (facing the top). Secure the backing in place by pushing the brass clips inwards.

The first row of long vertical stitches

CHART KEY • Small Landscape

Colour	Thread	Stitch
Sand	Anchor Nordin: 372 (2 str)	Long straight stitch
Stone	Anchor Nordin: 392 (2 str)	Long straight stitch
Blue green	Anchor Nordin: 215 (2 str)	Long straight stitch
Grass green	Anchor Nordin: 261 (2 str)	Long straight stitch
Avocado green	Anchor Nordin: 843 (2 str)	Long straight stitch
Dark emerald green	Anchor Nordin: 217 (2 str)	Long straight stitch
Dark red	Anchor Nordin: 47 (2 str)	French knot
Light red	Anchor Nordin: 13 (2 str)	French knot
Corn	Anchor Nordin: 391 (1 str)	Long diagonal stitch

Garden Gate

This design combines many of the techniques learned in previous chapters with the textural interest of knots and loops on the surface. The garden gate is stitched simply in backstitch and makes a focal point to the design. Outside this there is a patterned brick wall of long cross stitch, around which tall flowers grow and over which a wisteria bough curves gracefully. The little bushes and flowers in the foreground combine long cross stitch and french knots in different thicknesses of thread for greater textural interest.

YOU WILL NEED

The finished embroidery measures
12.5 cm x 14 cm (5 in x 5½ in)

35.5 cm x 45.5 cm (14 in x 16 in) bone 25-count
  Lugana evenweave fabric
Nos 22, 24 and 26 tapestry needles
Stranded cottons as listed on the colour key
Perle No 5 embroidery threads as listed on the
  colour key
Frame

STITCHING THE EMBROIDERY

1 Insert the fabric in a hoop or frame. One square of the chart represents two threads of the fabric in each direction. Use the number 22 tapestry needle for Perle No 5, the number 24 tapestry needle for three strands of stranded cotton, and the number 26 tapestry needle for one or two strands of stranded cotton. Following the chart and colour key, start stitching the area inside the garden gate in simple cross stitch using three strands of stranded cotton.

2 Stitch the garden path using a mixture of long cross stitches and simple cross stitches, arranged to form a pattern (over two rows which are then repeated). Follow the charts for stitch details. Read the symbols on the main chart carefully, as some shades appear more than once. Where you see a row of three symbols together, a long cross stitch over three squares is indicated. Check any pattern you are not sure of against the photographs.

3 To stitch the gardens to the left and right of the path, put the small clumps of flowers in place first. Start with the purple ones along the path edges and work the long crosses first. The pattern the long crosses make is shown on the charts. Work the areas around the flowers in long cross stitch over two squares. Start from the first row of the path. Where you have only one square left, put a simple cross stitch in it. Offset the rows by one square so that the long crosses do not start directly underneath each other.

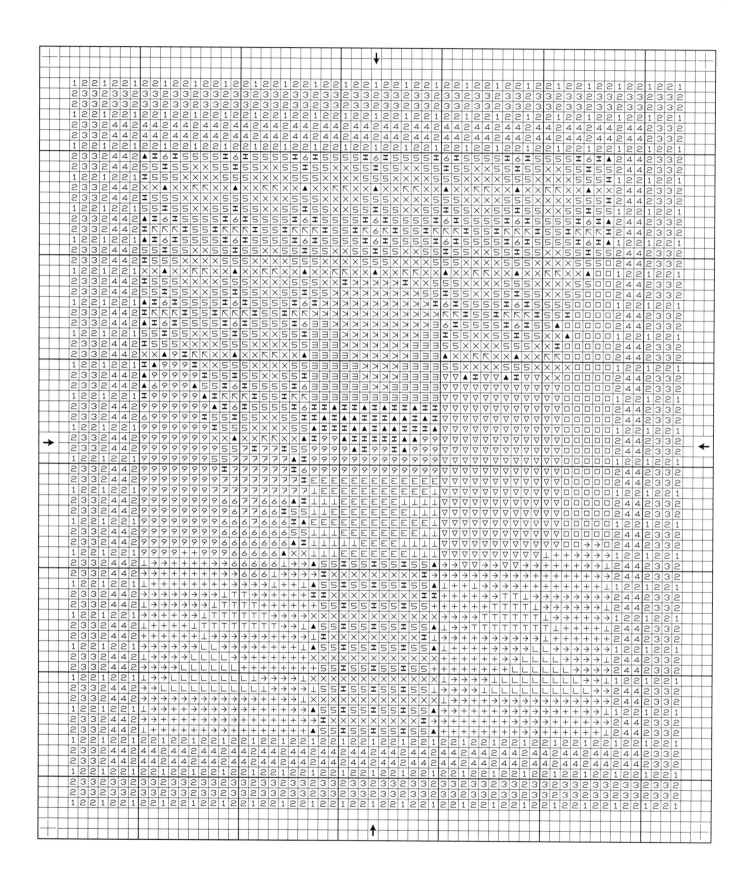

CHART KEY • Garden Gate

Symbol	Colour	Thread	Stitch
1	Emerald green	Anchor stranded cotton: 210 (3 str)	Simple cross stitch
2	Dark blue green	Anchor stranded cotton: 878 (3 str)	Long cross stitch
3	Blue green Raspberry pink	Anchor Perle No 5: 877 (1 str) Anchor stranded cotton: 68 (2 str)	Large cross stitch Large plus stitch
4	Pine green Apple green	Anchor Perle No 5: 262 (1 str) Anchor stranded cotton: 261 (2 str)	Large cross stitch Large plus stitch
E	Apple green	Anchor stranded cotton: 261 (3 str)	Simple cross stitch
6	Rust	Anchor stranded cotton: 349 (3 str)	Simple cross stitch
7	Dark grass green	Anchor stranded cotton: 266 (3 str)	Simple cross stitch
9	Dark pine green	Anchor stranded cotton: 268 (3 str)	Simple cross stitch
⋊	Sky blue	Anchor stranded cotton: 128 (3 str)	Simple cross stitch
+	Dark emerald green	Anchor Perle No 5: 212 (1 str)	Long cross stitch
⊥	Blue green	Anchor stranded cotton: 877 (3 str)	Simple cross stitch
▽	Apple green	Anchor stranded cotton: 261 (3 str)	Detached chain stitch
T	Grass green	Anchor Perle No 5: 265 (1 str)	Long cross stitch
→	Blue green	Anchor stranded cotton: 877 (3 str)	Long cross stitch
∟	Dark grass green	Anchor Perle No 5: 266 (1 str)	Long cross stitch
∃	Dark blue green	Anchor stranded cotton: 878 (3 str)	Simple cross stitch
▯	Dark pine green	Anchor stranded cotton: 268 (3 str)	Detached chain stitch
⤢	Rust	Anchor stranded cotton: 349 (3 str)	Long cross stitch
5	Golden sand	Anchor stranded cotton: 368 (3 str)	Long cross stitch
X	Light rust	Anchor stranded cotton: 369 (3 str)	Long cross stitch
⊥	Light rust	Anchor stranded cotton: 369 (3 str)	Simple cross stitch
▲	Golden sand	Anchor stranded cotton: 368 (3 str)	Simple cross stitch
	Dull brown	Anchor Perle No 5: 903 (1 str)	Couching (see chart detail, p 87)
	Dull brown	Anchor stranded cotton: 903 (1 str)	Simple cross stitch (see chart detail, p 87)

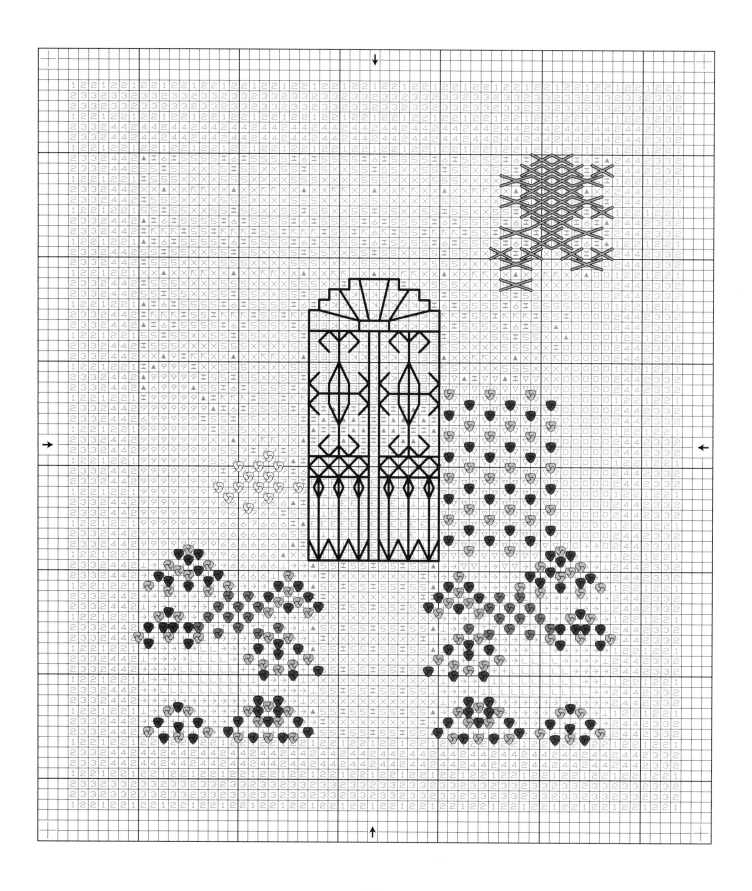

COLOUR CHART KEY • Garden Gate

Symbol	Colour	Thread	Stitch
——	Black	Anchor stranded cotton: 403 (1 str)	Backstitch
☉	Yellow	Anchor stranded cotton: 293 (3 str)	French knot
☉	Lavender	Anchor stranded cotton: 108 (3 str)	French knot
●	Purple	Anchor stranded cotton: 1030 (3 str)	French knot
☉	Light maroon	Anchor stranded cotton: 76 (3 str)	French knot
●	Dark maroon	Anchor stranded cotton: 78 (3 str)	French knot
☉	Grass green	Anchor stranded cotton: 265 (3 str)	French knot
══		Example of long cross stitch	

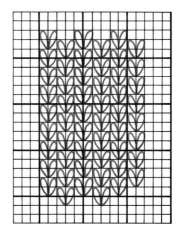

Detail of the tall flowers to the right of the gate

4 French knots are indicated on the charts by coloured knots. Refer to the photograph for the position of light and dark colours. Work the clumps that line the path alternately with lavender and purple. Work the outer clumps alternately with light and dark maroon. Decorate the upper of the two green clumps on either side of the plant with french knots in grass green. Decorate the lower of the two clumps of flowers on either side of the path with a pattern of detached chain stitches, using three strands of dark grass green.

5 Work the tall pot on the left of the wall and the conifer to the left of the pot in simple cross stitch. Work the plant in simple cross stitch, then add french knots in yellow using three strands of cotton in the needle where indicated by knots.

6 Work the tall flowers on the right of the gate in detached chain, worked in vertical rows with three strands of apple green (see the chart detail above). Work the french knots alternately with light maroon and maroon Perle No 5, starting at the top left with light maroon and working down in vertical rows where indicated by knots.

Detached chain stitch

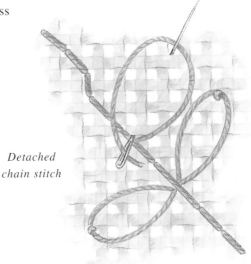

Detached chain stitch

*Detail of
the tall conifer*

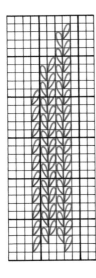

7 Work the tall conifer to the right of this area with three strands in simple cross stitch. Place detached chain stitches with one strand of pine green over this, as shown on the chart detail above.

8 Work the wall, following the chart and photograph, where it is shown most clearly. It contains simple cross stitches and long crosses as marked on the key. Watch out for the places where three symbols in a row indicate a long cross stitch three squares long.

9 Work the stem of the wisteria bough by couching a length of dull brown Perle No 5, with a strand of cotton in dull brown, where the thick continuous line and the x are indicated. The x has been used as a decorative way of catching down the Perle No 5.

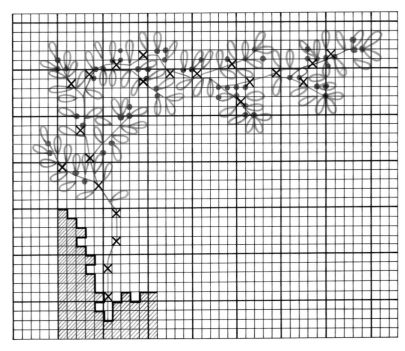

*Detail of the wisteria bough showing the position
of the french knots*

10 Work the leaves of the wisteria in three strands of grass green in detached chain stitch. Note the position of the inner row of the border, and count from there. Add the french knots using three strands of purple.

11 Work the border in two different rows which are repeated to form a pattern. The main chart (see page 84) shows that the inner row consists of a simple cross stitch (starting at any corner) and then a long cross stitch (worked over two rows). Repeat these all the way around the picture. Work the second and third rows of the border together as one. These consist of a double cross stitch and a long cross stitch, worked alternately around the border. The double cross stitch is made up of a large cross stitch with pine green Perle No 5 and a large plus stitch with two strands of apple green. Work the long cross stitch in three strands of dark blue green. The four squares together in a square represent the double cross

stitch, and are placed beside the long cross stitch from the first row. Place the long cross stitch where the short axis joins the first row.

12 Work the fourth row the same as the first row. The fifth row is a double row involving double cross stitch. Work the double cross stitch with a large cross stitch in blue green Perle no 5, with a large plus stitch over in two strands of raspberry pink. Alternate this with a long cross stitch as for rows 2 and 3. The final row is as the first row. This border could be adapted with different combinations of stitches and colours to form attractive patterns.

MOUNTING THE EMBROIDERY

Centre your embroidery over the frame's backing board, ensuring that the fabric threads run parallel with the edges of the board. Lace the back of the embroidery and place the board back into the frame (see page 124).

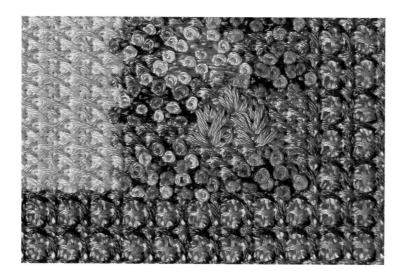

Semi-sheer Fabrics

Using semi-sheer fabrics in cross stitch embroidery adds a new dimension to your work. It allows you to add instant colour and depth to a design without stitching the whole area. Yet, because the fabric is almost transparent, you can count the threads underneath and stitch on top.

Using fine fabric woven from such a thin thread that you can see through it, is a quick and easy way of emphasizing part of a design. The semi-sheer fabrics used here have the advantage of being colourful and allow you to count the threads of fabric underneath. The main advantage of this is to give depth to a design, but it has the added advantage of providing an area which does not need stitching. In this design I have compromised with stitching some areas in cross stitch, and adding sparkle with long straight stitches in others. I hope you enjoy working this new technique; it is certainly a way of adding instant colour to a design.

Waterfall

I have used the overlays in part of the design area, but you could use the same technique to enhance a plain fabric by covering the design area completely. For small projects such as greetings cards this is inexpensive, and can bring an element of mystery into your work.

YOU WILL NEED

The finished card measures 5 cm x 7.5 cm (2 in x 3 in)

9 cm (3¹/₂ in) square of leaf green semi-sheer fabric
15 cm (6 in) square of sky blue 18-count Aida fabric
Basting cotton
Nos 24 and 26 tapestry needles
Stranded cottons as listed on the colour key
5 cm x 7.5 cm (2 in x 3 in) small oval card (see page 127 for suppliers)

STITCHING THE EMBROIDERY

1 Place the semi-sheer square over the centre of the Aida fabric and baste it in place along the horizontal centre line and the vertical centre line. Then baste around the edges. Insert the fabric in a hoop or frame. Use the number 26 tapestry needle for single stranded work and a number 24 tapestry needle for two-thread work.

2 Stitch the counted cross stitch areas with one strand of stranded cotton. Stitch up to the edge of the design at the top and the lower edge, leaving the last squares of the design

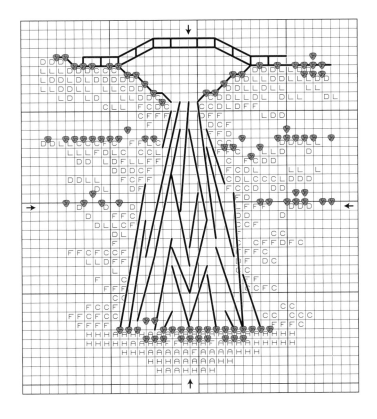

unstitched. Trim the semi-sheer fabric close to these stitches, and then stitch the last row over the raw edges.

3 Now work the backstitch outlines. Outline the bridge with dark brown and the top of the grass with dark green. Stitch the long diagonal lines with two strands of white. Work long diagonal stitches between these white stitches, filling in the gaps with one strand of pale grey and one strand of dark grey. Then go over the white stitches again to raise up the waterfall area of the design.

4 Finally work the french knots. Work those at the foot of the waterfall with one strand of white, and those at the top of the waterfall and elsewhere with two strands of dark green.

MOUNTING THE EMBROIDERY

Trim the semi-sheer fabric back to about 1 cm (½ in) from the edge of the design, then mount it into the presentation card, following the instructions on page 25.

CHART KEY • Waterfall

Symbol	Colour	Thread	Stitch
A	White	Anchor stranded cotton: 1 (1 str)	Simple cross stitch
C	Pale grey	Anchor stranded cotton: 232 (1 str)	Simple cross stitch
D	Grass green	Anchor stranded cotton: 265 (1 str)	Simple cross stitch
L	Dark grass green	Anchor stranded cotton: 266 (1 str)	Simple cross stitch
F	Dark grey	Anchor stranded cotton: 235 (1 str)	Simple cross stitch
	White	Anchor stranded cotton: 1 (2 str)	Long diagonal stitch
	Dark brown	Anchor stranded cotton: 380 (1 str)	Backstitch
	Dark green	Anchor stranded cotton: 268 (1 str)	Backstitch
	Pale grey	Anchor stranded cotton: 232 (1 str)	Long stitch
	Dark grey	Anchor stranded cotton: 235 (1 str)	Long stitch
	White	Anchor stranded cotton: 1 (1 str)	French knot
	Dark green	Anchor stranded cotton: 268 (2 str)	French knot
H	Blue	Anchor stranded cotton: 920 (1 str)	Simple cross stitch

Lily Pond

This design is another of my garden fantasies. The coolness of the pond with its floating water-lilies is further emphasized by the architectural features of the garden beyond. The waters are created by laying down semi-sheer fabrics, which are broken up into smaller shapes by embroidering over areas in simple cross stitch. The variety of garden flowers, foliage and trees makes this a complex and fascinating project both to work and to admire when complete.

YOU WILL NEED

The finished design measures 22.5 cm x 19.5 cm (8⅞ in x 7¾ in)

Semi-sheer fabrics as listed on the colour key
40 cm (15¾ in) square of sky blue 28-count
  Brittney evenweave fabric
Basting cotton
Nos 24 and 26 tapestry needles
Stranded cottons as listed on the colour key
Blending filaments as listed on the colour key
Frame

STITCHING THE EMBROIDERY

1 Before starting work, position the semi-sheer overlays in place on the Aida fabric. The two areas where the first semi-sheer fabric is to be placed are outlined by a black line on the chart. Lay down the darker greeny-blue semi-sheer fabric over these small areas. Baste in place, then trim the fabric around the shapes a little outside the basted line on the stitched edges. These edges will be stitched over by cross stitches.

2 Lay the paler greeny-blue semi-sheer fabric over the whole area of the pond (including the two small areas previously applied) and baste in position. Trim away the edges close to the pond margins as before.

3 One square of the chart represents one simple cross stitch and two threads of the fabric in both directions. Stitch the lily plants floating in the middle of the pond. These will help to keep the fabric anchored in place. Then stitch the areas outside the pond by counting from the central lily plant towards the large urn, and work these areas. Work around the pond margins, stitching the raw edges of the semi-sheer fabric under your cross stitch. Take out the basting stitches as you reach them. This is best achieved from the back of your work for the underneath layers of fabric.

4 Now work the ripples on the pond. Use one strand of sparkling green blending filament to make the ripple patterns on the darker areas. Use two strands of sparkling pale blue to make the ripple patterns in the paler area. Use one strand of sparkling bright blue in both areas.

5 The ripple patterns are simple. Use the illustration as a guide, and work similar patterns in the pond area. I have worked the area quite intensively, but you can leave more areas blank if you wish.

6 Now work the main design in simple cross stitch. Outline the sun dial, the steps, and the temple with backstitch in dark grey. Work the tall grasses in long straight stitches in two

colours. Work the darker shade with two strands of apple green and the lighter shade with grass green. I have used grass green as the lighter shade for most of the grasses, but for variation, I have used avocado green for some of the grasses. These are the three clumps on the extreme right at the lower edge of the picture, and also the three clumps to the left of the urn. Work the long grasses under the urn with one strand of grass green. Work the french knots over the urn with one strand of

dark blue green. Work the french knots on the upper bank with two strands of bright yellow.

MOUNTING THE EMBROIDERY

Centre your embroidery over the frame's backing board, ensuring that the fabric threads run parallel with the edges of the board. Lace the back of the embroidery and place the board back into the frame (see page 124).

CHART KEY • Lily Pond

Symbol	Colour	Thread	Stitch
▼	Pale lavender	Anchor stranded cotton: 117 (2 str)	Simple cross stitch
II	White	Anchor stranded cotton: 1 (2 str)	Simple cross stitch
=	Blue green Pale emerald green	Anchor stranded cotton: 876 (1 str) Anchor stranded cotton: 208 (1 str)	Simple cross stitch
1	Pink	Anchor stranded cotton: 75 (2 str)	Simple cross stitch
2	Dark sand	Anchor stranded cotton: 373 (2 str)	Simple cross stitch
Ø	Off white	Anchor stranded cotton: 926 (2 str)	Simple cross stitch
4	Grass green	Anchor stranded cotton: 265 (2 str)	Simple cross stitch
5	Mid yellow	Anchor stranded cotton: 293 (2 str)	Simple cross stitch
6	Pale emerald green	Anchor stranded cotton: 208 (2 str)	Simple cross stitch
7	Dull brown	Anchor stranded cotton: 898 (2 str)	Simple cross stitch
8	Dark pink	Anchor stranded cotton: 76 (2 str)	Simple cross stitch
9	Pale yellow stone	Anchor stranded cotton: 885 (2 str)	Simple cross stitch
◤	Lavender	Anchor stranded cotton: 118 (2 str)	Simple cross stitch
◸	Dark blue green	Anchor stranded cotton: 878 (2 str)	Simple cross stitch
E	Mid blue green	Anchor stranded cotton: 877 (2 str)	Simple cross stitch
M	Pale pink	Anchor stranded cotton: 73 (2 str)	Simple cross stitch
⊥	Light grass green	Anchor stranded cotton: 264 (2 str)	Simple cross stitch
⅂	Brightest green	Anchor stranded cotton: 258 (2 str)	Simple cross stitch
//	Brown	Anchor stranded cotton: 358 (2 str)	Simple cross stitch
/	Dark blue green Pale emerald green	Anchor stranded cotton: 878 (1 str) Anchor stranded cotton: 208 (1 str)	Simple cross stitch
J	Terracotta	Anchor stranded cotton: 339 (2 str)	Simple cross stitch
V	Sand	Anchor stranded cotton: 372 (2 str)	Simple cross stitch
I	Pale lavender Lavender	Anchor stranded cotton: 117(1 str) Anchor stranded cotton: 118 (1 str)	Simple cross stitch
X	Pale pink Pink	Anchor stranded cotton: 73 (1 str) Anchor stranded cotton: 75 (1str)	Simple cross stitch
W	Blue green	Anchor stranded cotton: 876 (2 str)	Simple cross stitch
K	Apple green	Anchor stranded cotton: 261 (2 str)	Simple cross stitch

(continued on page 96)

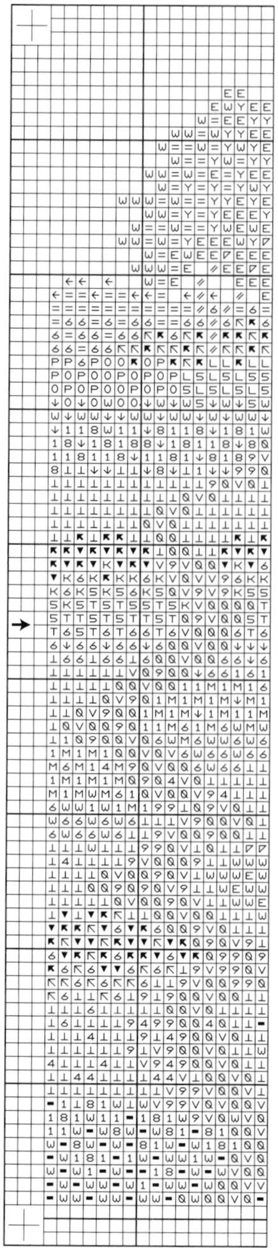

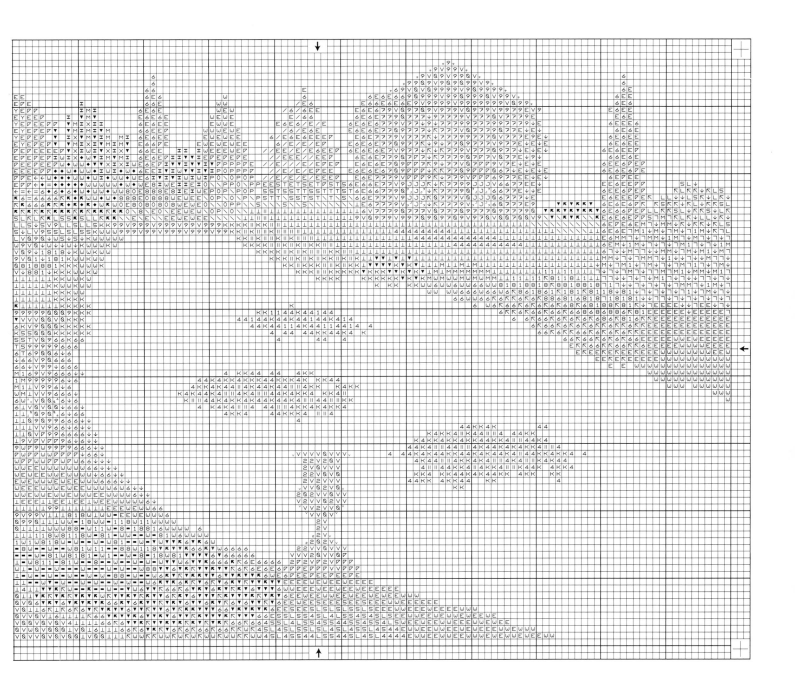

CHART KEY • Lily Pond *(continued)*

Symbol	Colour	Thread	Stitch
L	Pale yellow	Anchor stranded cotton: 292 (2 str)	Simple cross stitch
T	Bright yellow	Anchor stranded cotton: 295 (2 str)	Simple cross stitch
←	Blue green	Anchor stranded cotton: 876 (1 str)	Simple cross stitch
↖	Bright green	Anchor stranded cotton: 244 (2 str)	Simple cross stitch
O	Light maroon	Anchor stranded cotton: 78 (2 str)	Simple cross stitch
Y	Bright green Mid blue green	Anchor stranded cotton: 244 (1 str) Anchor stranded cotton: 877 (1 str)	Simple cross stitch
P	Light maroon Dark pink	Anchor stranded cotton :78 (1 str) Anchor stranded cotton: 76 (1 str)	Simple cross stitch
\	Dark grass green	Anchor stranded cotton: 267 (2 str)	Simple cross stitch
■	Light blue green	Anchor stranded cotton: 875 (2 str)	Simple cross stitch
↓	Light bright green	Anchor stranded cotton: 242 (2 str)	Simple cross stitch
◆	Blue green Apple green	Anchor stranded cotton: 876 (1 str) Anchor stranded cotton: 261 (1 str)	Simple cross stitch

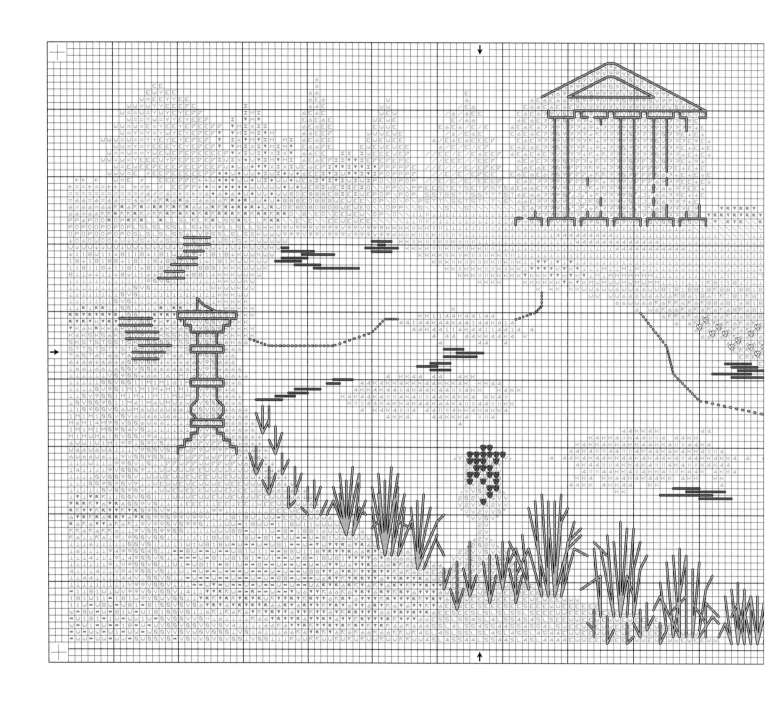

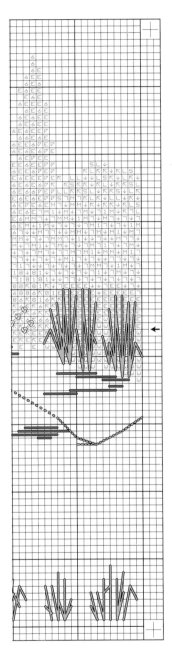

COLOUR CHART KEY • Lily Pond

Symbol	Colour	Thread	Stitch
—	Dark grey	Anchor stranded cotton: 400 (1 str)	Backstitch
—	Sparkling green	Kreinik blending filament: K029 (1 str)	Straight stitch
and	Sparkling pale blue	Kreinik blending filament: K094 (2 str)	Straight stitch
and	Sparkling bright blue	Kreinik blending filament: K014H1 (1 str)	Straight stitch
—	Apple green	Anchor stranded cotton: 261 (2 str)	Long straight stitch
and	Grass green	Anchor stranded cotton: 265 (2 str)	Long straight stitch
and	Avocado green	Anchor stranded cotton: 843 (2 str)	Long straight stitch
✾	Bright yellow	Anchor stranded cotton: 295 (2 str)	French knot
❧	Dark blue green	Anchor stranded cotton: 878 (1 str)	French knot
∘∘∘∘	Edge of transparent fabric		

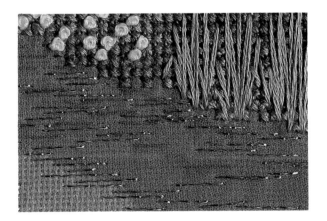

Simple Goldwork

Goldwork is one of the more advanced techniques in the embroiderer's
repertoire. In this chapter the simplest goldwork technique of
laying down gold threads on a dark fabric background, and attaching them
with patterns of stitches is introduced.

At its best goldwork is heavenly, and I use the word advisedly as goldwork was traditionally used for ecclesiastical vestments. At one time, English embroiderers led the world in the craft of goldwork. Gold threads were imported from Venice, we laboured over beautiful copes, and then sent them to Rome.

With the technology currently used in thread manufacture you do not have to be a professional embroiderer to tackle simple goldwork. The main thread manufacturers all make a variety of threads which are much easier to use than those of medieval craftsmen – and you can purchase them from your local craft store.

In this chapter I have taken the simplest goldwork technique of laying down gold threads over a dark background fabric, and attaching them by stitching coloured patterns over the thicker gold threads. If that sounds familiar it is because the actual goldwork technique is the same in essence as the technique of couching, which was introduced on page 36.

Butterfly Picture

The design is worked by laying down gold threads, and securing them in place decoratively with simple cross stitch. The cross stitch is worked using a single strand of stranded cotton to allow the gold thread to show through. The overall effect of this piece is as though you had cross stitched on to a piece of gold cloth. The chart shows the position of the cross stitches. You will note that half crosses appear around the edge of the design in some places to give a delicate edge to the butterfly's wings.

YOU WILL NEED

The finished embroidery measures
7 cm x 5.5 cm (2¾ in x 2¼ in)

20 cm (8 in) square of ash rosa 25-count Davosa
* evenweave fabric*
Light gold thread as listed on the colour key
Pins
Nos 20 and 26 tapestry needles
Stranded cottons as listed on the colour key
10 cm (4 in) wooden circular frame

STITCHING THE EMBROIDERY

1 Insert the fabric in a hoop or frame. One square of the chart represents two threads of the fabric in each direction. Work the first row by cutting a piece of light gold thread measuring 15 cm (6 in) and pinning this on to the centre of the fabric horizontally. This will be the middle row of your chart. The gold thread lies in the middle of the squares in the central rows horizontally across the chart, and the cross stitches are stitched over it. Work the cross stitches with a number 26 tapestry needle. Leave the ends on the front of your fabric. Cut another piece of gold thread the same length for the row above and stitch over it as above; this will be row 2. Continue in this way until you have stitched four rows.

2 Using the number 20 tapestry needle, take the loose ends of the gold thread through to the back of the work to secure. On rows 1 and 3 take the gold thread through the centre hole of the square, because these are half stitches. On rows 2 and 4 take the thread through the hole on the right-hand edge of the centre of the square, for the stitches on the right-hand edge of the design, and on the left for the other side. Neaten the raw edges of thread by stitching back into the area of the design on the reverse with small stitches over the loose ends of gold thread. When you have stitched four or five stitches, snip away the excess gold, and continue for the other three rows.

3 Continue stitching in this way, working rows 15-22 inclusively. Rows 23 and 24 require you to count to the centre of the butterfly, and stitch the gold for the squares through the fabric without cross stitches in the centre of the design, and come up for the small abdominal area, back down again, and then up for the right-hand wing.

4 Work the remaining rows of the design at the lower and upper edges with gold lengths of 11 cm (4⅜ in) on the left and on the right of the design (one length for each wing.) This means you have to work the wings on the left individually, and then the wings on the right. Remember to neaten the ends after every four rows on the reverse. For the very tips of the wings at the top and the lower edge you will need to work the ends diagonally into the design area. Complete the design by working the antennae with one strand of dark brown, and work the top two squares three times for a fuller effect on each side. Goldwork is often padded slightly from behind the work to give the sparkling threads a chance to really catch the light.

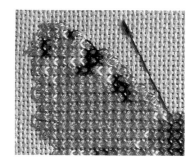

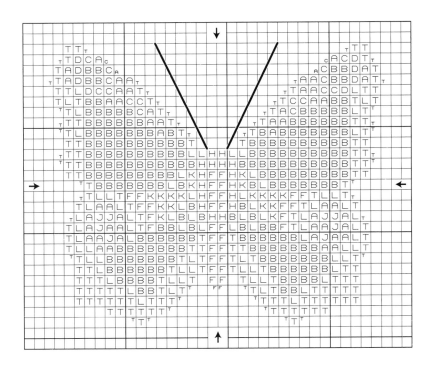

MOUNTING THE EMBROIDERY

When the embroidery is complete it will be most effective to use the wadding in the frame kit to raise the embroidery slightly. You may decide not to use the glass in the frame as it decreases the effect of the gold thread. Complete the mounting of the embroidery in the frame as for the poppy field design on page 79, but cut a circle of thin card to encase the embroidery instead of using the paper provided.

CHART KEY • Butterfly Picture

Gold Thread, Maderia: 3003, is laid down under every row.

Symbol	Colour	Thread	Stitch
A	Black	Anchor stranded cotton: 403 (1 str)	Simple cross stitch
B	Terracotta	Anchor stranded cotton: 339 (1 str)	Simple cross stitch
C	Yellow	Anchor stranded cotton: 293 (1 str)	Simple cross stitch
D	Purple	Anchor stranded cotton: 118 (1 str)	Simple cross stitch
T	Dark sand	Anchor stranded cotton: 374 (1 str)	Simple cross stitch
F	Dark brown	Anchor stranded cotton: 381 (1 str)	Simple cross stitch
L	Light sand	Anchor stranded cotton: 372 (1 str)	Simple cross stitch
H	Chestnut brown	Anchor stranded cotton: 357 (1 str)	Simple cross stitch
J	Dark purple	Anchor stranded cotton: 119 (1 str)	Simple cross stitch
K	Light chestnut brown	Anchor stranded cotton: 944 (1 str)	Simple cross stitch
	Dark brown	Anchor stranded cotton: 381 (1 str)	Backstitch

Sampler

This sampler is designed to show the richness and variety of effects achieved by using only the simplest techniques of goldwork. The threads employed complement each other perfectly. The blending filament is easy to couch, yet gives depth and splendour to the shiny golds. The beads and sequins make a textural change that enhances the pattern elements.

YOU WILL NEED

The finished embroidery measures 10.5 cm (4¼ in) square

30 cm (12 in) square of black 27-count Linda
  evenweave fabric
Nos 26, 24 and 20 tapestry needles
Beading straw
Stranded cottons as listed on the colour key
Light gold thread as listed on the colour key
Astrella gold thread as listed on the colour key
Blending filaments as listed on the colour key
Ophir gold thread as listed on the colour key
Beads and sequins as listed on the colour key
Rayon threads as listed on the colour key

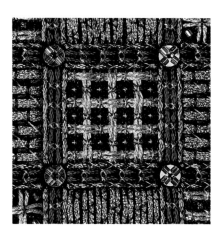

STITCHING THE EMBROIDERY

1 Insert the fabric in a hoop or frame. One square of the chart represents two threads of fabric in both directions. Following the chart, count out to the first turquoise square outline in the centre of the design. By placing the turquoise outlines on first you will find counting the gold squares within them easy. The turquoise squares are laid down by couching. Use a number 20 needle to lay the threads, a number 24 needle for two strands of stranded cotton thread, and a number 26 needle for blending filament. Using the thread whole, make one long stitch for each side of the squares. When laying down the rayon threads, the thread lies between the two threads of the fabric that make up one square of the chart. Leave a loose end 2.5 cm (1 in) long at the back of the fabric, and pin it away from your stitching. This will be secured later.
2 Work the long cross stitches over the turquoise square, as shown in the chart, using yellow gold blending thread. Loop the thread around the eye of the needle for ease of stitching.
3 Work the maroon colour in two rows around the turquoise square. Then work small simple cross stitches to secure them using Ophir gold thread without stranding down. Check your work against the chart. Now place the remaining turquoise squares in place, and work these in the same way, using two rows of maroon thread between them each time. Finally, place one large turquoise square

around the whole design, and secure with long cross stitches.

4 Work each of the square fillings in the same manner as the grid. Lay down gold threads, placing them as before, between two threads of the fabric making up each square of the chart. Then secure them with finer threads; finally take the ends of gold thread through to the back of your work using the size 20 tapestry needle, and secure. Each square except the central one is repeated.

5 To work the central square, use Madeira light gold and place the thread as shown on the chart. Place the horizontal threads first, and weave the vertical ones in and out. When placing these threads, work the first of each pair first or a gap will appear where the second thread returns (see the diagram below).

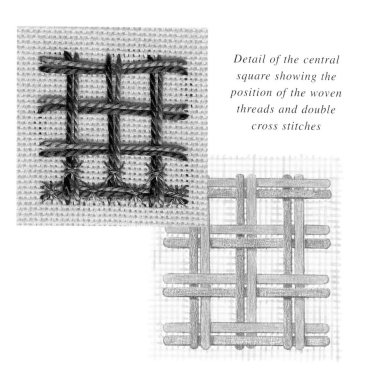

Detail of the central square showing the position of the woven threads and double cross stitches

6 Decorate the horizontal pairs of thread with double cross stitches made up of a large cross stitch with one strand of dark turquoise. Stitch the large plus stitch with Ophir used whole. Decorate the vertical rows of light gold with double cross stitches made up of a large cross stitch with one strand of navy, and a large plus stitch with light gold blending filament. Place small plus stitches in the centre of the black squares with one strand of light turquoise.

7 Work the top left and lower right square next. Place horizontal rows of Madeira light gold and decorate them with double cross stitches made up of a large cross stitch with one strand of light turquoise, and a large plus stitch with light gold blending filament unstranded. Place a double cross stitch in the black rows between these, made up of a small cross stitch with one strand of light turquoise. Work the small plus stitch with one strand of light gold blending filament (see the chart for the stitch position).

8 Now work the top and lower middle squares. Lay down rows of Astrella gold thread vertically (as illustrated in step 5) and decorate these with fly stitches on their sides (see the illustrations on page 107) using one strand of navy.

9 Then work the top right and lower left square. Lay down vertical rows of Madeira light gold, and then place horizontal rows on top. Decorate these with double cross stitches where the threads cross. Work the large cross stitch with one strand of light turquoise, and a large plus stitch with one strand of navy. Place turquoise embroidery beads in the centre of the

106

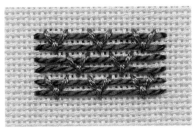

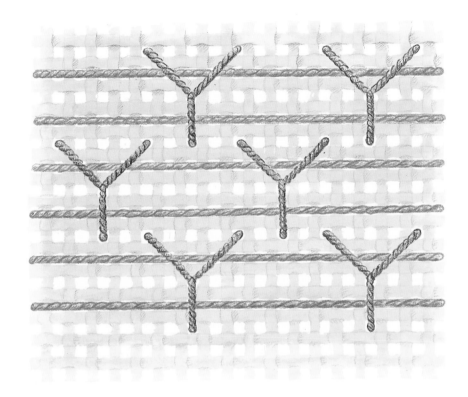

Fly stitch in position over the laid threads

black squares, using a beading straw and one strand of light turquoise where indicated by diagonal lines on the chart.

10 To work the middle left and middle right square, place horizontal rows of Astrella gold as shown in chart 2. Decorate these with a stepped pattern using two strands of navy stranded cotton, and diagonal stitches of one strand of light turquoise.

11 Place the sequins and gold beads where the rayon thread squares meet. Position the sequin with a pin. Thread a beading straw with one strand of navy and come up from the centre of the square, thread a gold embroidery bead on to the straw and go back down at the top right of the square. Come back up through the centre, thread on a gold bead and go back down at the top left of the square. Continue in this way until all four beads have been stitched in place. Repeat at the intersections of all the squares.

MOUNTING THE EMBROIDERY

Centre your embroidery over the frame's backing board, ensuring that the fabric threads run parallel with the edges of the board. Lace the back of the embroidery and place the board back into the frame (see page 124).

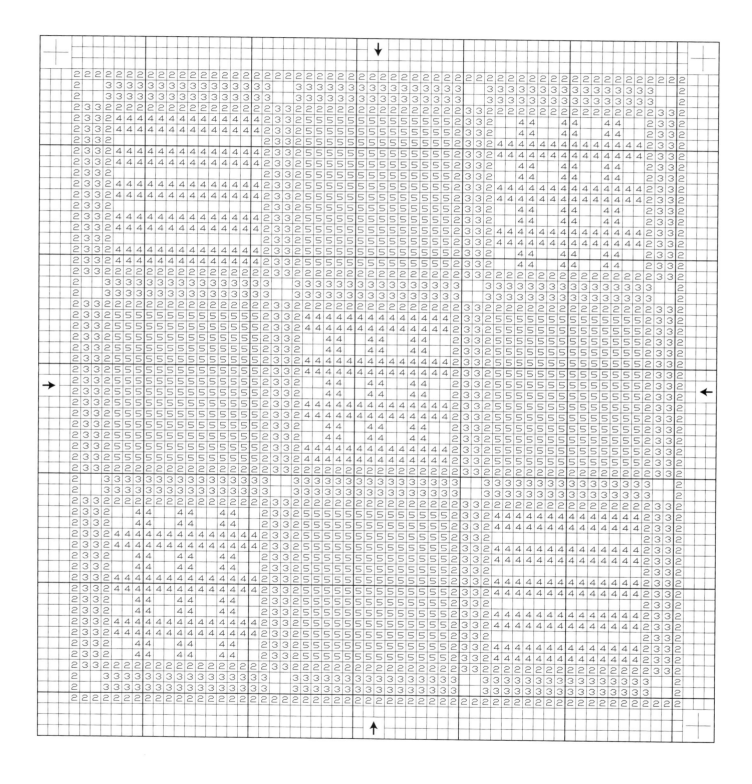

CHART KEY • Sampler

Symbol	Colour	Thread	Stitch
Grid squares			
2	Turquoise	Anchor Marlitt: 1055	Long stitch
3	Maroon	Anchor Marlitt: 844	Long stitch
Centre square			
4	Light gold	Maderia: 3003	Long stitch
Left top and lower right square			
4	Light gold	Maderia: 3003	Long stitch
Top middle and lower middle square			
5	Gold	Coats Astrella	Long vertical stitch
Top right and lower left square			
4	Light gold	Maderia: 3003	Long straight stitch
Middle left and middle right square			
5	Gold	Coats Astrella	Long horizontal stitch

COLOUR CHART KEY • Sampler

Symbol	Colour	Thread	Stitch
Grid squares			
▭	Yellow gold	Kreinik blending filament: 002J (1 str)	Long cross stitch (shown as long cross on chart
▭	Gold	Coats Ophir	Small cross stitch (shown as cross on chart)
Centre square			
—	Dark turquoise Gold	Anchor stranded cotton: 169 (1 str) Coats Ophir	Large cross Large plus
—	Navy Light gold	Anchor stranded cotton: 164 (1 str) Kreinik cable: 002P	Large cross Large plus
—	Light turquoise	Anchor stranded cotton: 168	Small plus stitch
Top left and lower right square			
—	Light turquoise Light gold	Anchor stranded cotton: 168 (1 str) Kreinik cable: 002P	Large cross Large plus
—	Light turquoise Light gold	Anchor stranded cotton: 168 (1 str) Kreinik cord: 002C	Small cross Small plus
Top middle and lower middle square			
—	Navy	Anchor stranded cotton: 164 (1 str)	Fly stitch (on its side)
Top right and lower left square			
—	Light turquoise Navy	Anchor stranded cotton: 168 (1 str) Anchor stranded cotton: 164 (1 str)	Large cross Large plus
—	Light turquoise Turquoise	Anchor stranded cotton: 168 (1 str) Embroidery bead	Diagonal stitch
Middle left and middle right square			
—	Navy	Anchor stranded cotton: 164 (2 str)	Stepped backstitch
—	Light turquoise	Anchor stranded cotton: 168 (1 str)	Diagonal stitch
Sequins and beads			
—	Navy Dior blue Gold	Anchor stranded cotton: 164 (1 str) 6mm sequin Embroidery bead	Straight stitch

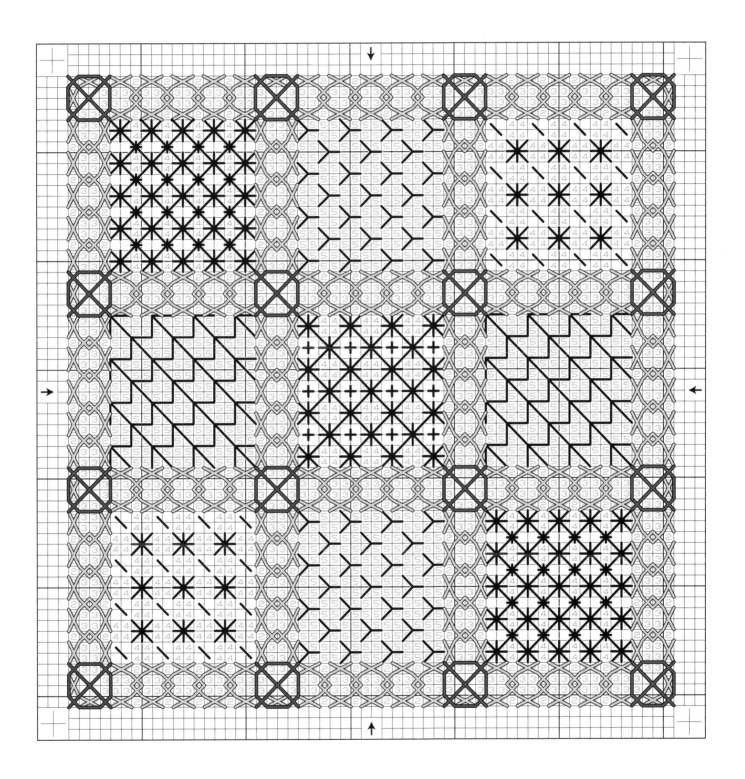

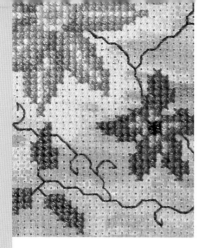

Painting
and Dyeing

*Colouring your background fabric with paint or dye can give you a
more interesting surface on which to embroider, and means that you do not
have to cover the whole area with stitching. You can paint a wash of pale
colour, or you can use a stencil to create self-contained areas of colour.*

By using watercolour fabric dyes it is possible
to create a naturalistic background for flower
beds, a watery effect for ponds and seascapes
or, as in the case of our main project, a wall
effect as a background to climbing plants. One
of the most simple effects that can be achieved
by dyeing is that of stencilling. To stencil your
fabric, first ensure that the stencil is placed
squarely on the counted fabric. Stencil the
colours on to the fabric and leave to dry. Set
with an iron, if necessary. Then take a couple
of shades of stranded cotton, one a little lighter
than the stencilled colour, and one a little
darker. Make a cross stitch pattern in the

stencilled area for a graphic effect, or highlight
a detail of the stencilled area if the main
design is too linear.

Using watercolour paints instead of fabric
paints and dyes can still achieve a good colour
effect, but it is not possible to set the paints in
the same way. You also need to be careful not
to wet the fabric after the paint has dried, and
not to wash the embroidery after completion.

You could also use water-soluble pencils in
the same way as paint, mixing the colours on
the fabric. These are more difficult to manage,
however, because you may have to wet the area
and re-apply colour several times.

Tulip Tray Cloth

This design is particularly useful if you want to have the effect of a colour change; here parrot tulips change colour from dark pink to light pink. It is an adaptable design which could be used in many colourways to suit different furnishings. The thread used is space dyed, which means that it is darker in some places than others. There are many other colours of space-dyed threads available, so you can choose one that fits in with your decorating scheme.

The tulip stencil

YOU WILL NEED

The finished tray cloth measures 42 cm x 33 cm (16½ in x 13 in), including fringe

Tracing paper
Pencil
Stencil card
Newspaper
Masking tape
Stencil paints in avocado green and raspberry pink
Stencil brush
51 cm x 38 cm (20 in x 15 in) ivory 27-count Linda evenweave fabric
No 24 tapestry needle
Stranded cottons as listed on the colour key
Sewing thread to match fabric

PREPARING THE FABRIC

1 Trace the outline of the tulip design (see opposite) on to stencil card to achieve the design as shown, and cut out the shapes within the outlines using a pair of small sharp scissors.

2 Wash the evenweave fabric to remove any dressing which might impede the absorbency of the paint. Dry and iron the fabric. Baste the edge of the finished cloth in place or, if preferred, pull the thread around this edge. Place newspaper on a working surface, then put a piece of clean paper on top. Place the fabric on top of the clean paper and secure at the corners with masking tape. This will prevent any movement of the fabric during painting.

3 Read the instructions on the paint pots carefully before starting to stencil. Dip a stencil brush lightly in the pot of paint three or four times. Then dab it on a spare piece of paper to see how much paint you have on the brush. If the colour is very dark, dab more paint off the brush before using it on the fabric. Position the stencil on the fabric so that the right-hand edge of the design is 5cm (2in) from the edge of the cloth (including the

frayed edge). Stencil the tulip in raspberry pink, and the stem in avocado green. When you have completed this stage, leave the paint to dry for at least 24 hours. Iron the fabric on the back to set the paint. It is now washable.

STITCHING THE EMBROIDERY

Insert the fabric in a hoop or frame. One square of the chart represents two threads of the fabric in both directions. Following the chart, work the tulip petals with simple cross stitch in pink, and the leaves with green. As the thread is space dyed, it is darker in some places than others. Decide which areas you would like to be dark, and which light, and stitch accordingly.

FINISHING THE CLOTH

Trim the cloth to the finished size and pull out one thread all the way around about 20 threads in from the edge. This marks the hem edge. Finish the cloth by making a half cross stitch in a matching thread over two threads of fabric and two threads apart on the edge of the fabric all the way around. At the corners stitch diagonally into the corner. If the fabric proves to have an odd number of threads, miss one thread to make the pattern fit the corner. An alternative method of finishing is to machine zigzag with a small stitch all around the edge.

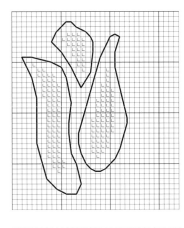
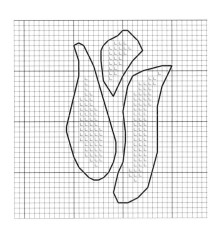
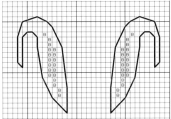
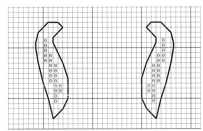

CHART KEY • Traycloth

Symbol	Colour	Thread	Stitch
L	Pink	Anchor: 1207 (2 str)	Simple cross stitch
B	Green	Anchor: 1216 (2 str)	Simple cross stitch

Cat and Clematis

This panel is designed with a lot of fun in mind. Painting the fabric with water-based dyes is quick and easy, giving a base to stitch on that makes something well known suddenly become experimental.

The size of the large clematis flowers is unexpected, and the colour of the smaller ones is very unusual. Only the black and white cat is predictable. The thatched roof is stitched in simple vertical stitches which overlap by two squares at the upper edge, making it quick to stitch but texturally interesting.

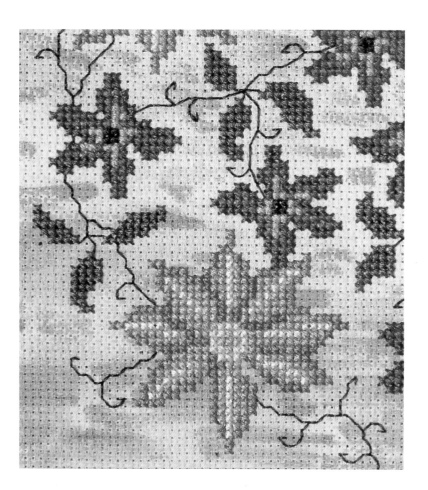

YOU WILL NEED

The finished embroidery measures 19.5 cm x 21.5 cm (7¾ in x 8½ in)

40 cm (15¾ in) square of white 16-count Aida fabric
Fabric dyes
Paintbrush
Nos 20, 24 and 26 tapestry needles
Stranded cottons as listed on the colour key
Perle cottons as listed on the colour key

DYEING THE FABRIC

1 One square of the chart represents one block of Aida fabric. Counting from the centre of the design, baste the outside edge of the grid area of the chart. This is the total area to be dyed. Baste the bottom line of the thatched roof with large stitches. You now have two areas to be dyed in slightly different colours.

2 I have used a paintbox selection of dyes; for suppliers see page 127. For the thatch area, mix 1 part Yellow No 12, 2 parts Yellow ochre No 6, 1 part White No 29 and ½ part Prussian blue No 24. Add the blue gradually as you may not need it all. Once mixed, it should be similar in shade to yellow ochre, roughly equivalent to DMC stranded cotton 3827.

3 For the lower wall area mix 2 parts Yellow Ochre No 6, 1 part Brown No 8, 1 part White No 29, and ½ part Prussian blue No 24. Add the blue gradually as you may not want to use it all. Once mixed, this dye should be a pale brick colour, roughly equivalent to DMC stranded cotton 3779.

4 Try out the colours on a scrap of fabric. Notice the colour and the thickness of the dye. Add more water to make it fluid, but be careful not to add too much or the dye may seep into another area. When you are happy with the consistency of the dye, paint the area at the top of the design representing the thatched roof with the yellow ochre mix. If you are not sure whether you have mixed enough dye, paint the dye on the fabric in areas 2.5 cm (1 in) apart. In this way, if you need more dye you can mix up more and it does not matter if the resulting colour is not exactly the same, you will just have a dappled effect on the fabric. The overall effect will be of long stitches of Perle threads over a yellow ochre-based fabric. The colour of the fabric will not be directly seen in this area.

5 Now dye the lower wall area. Remember that the overall effect required here is of a wall made up of different stones. To do this, split the dye up into three separate parts and then add an extra 1 part of dye to each separate part. Into the first pot put a little more yellow ochre. Into the second put a little more brown. Into the last put a little more white. Add a little more white to each shade until you have a pleasing mixture of shades. Lay the thread colours on to the fabric beside your dye pots and look at the strength of the dye. The dye should be paler than dark brick, but no paler than pale brick. If you are not sure whether this is so, half close your eyes and look at the dyes and threads again. This should reduce what you see to tones, rather that colours. If you are afraid to commit your brush to fabric,

try putting a very pale wash on first and gradually add more colour to the design. If your house is not made of the same colour building material, and you want to make the design more personal, add more brown, yellow ochre, or white, until you have a reasonable copy of the colour of your house. Apply the three dyes in areas about 2.5 cm (1 in) long and 2 cm (3/4 in) deep, varying the size of the stones slightly from time to time to make a pleasant composition.

6 Once the fabric is dyed, leave it to dry and then set with a steam iron. To set, place a clean sheet of white paper on the fabric and move the iron around over the paper every five seconds or so, until all the areas have been heated two or three times. Do not iron back and forth or leave the iron in the same place for too long, as this will affect the finish. When the steam has set the dye it should be permanent.

STITCHING THE EMBROIDERY

1 Insert the fabric in a hoop or frame. Then work the simple cross stitch first using two strands of stranded cotton in the needle and following the chart. The face of the cat contains some half stitches around the eyes, nose and mouth.

2 Now work the backstitch outlines. Outline the cat in black. Outline the face detail in black, except for the whiskers which are worked in white, with long straight stitches. Work the stems and tendrils of the clematis, and the stems of the pot geranium in very dark

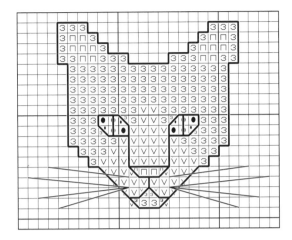

Detail of cat's face

green. Outline the windowsill along the horizontal with stone. Work the window panes with three strands of blue tones in long diagonal stitches. Complete all the panes in the same way.

3 Work the thatched roof with long straight stitches that overlap with two squares between each row. Begin at the left-hand edge of the fabric, and the lower edge of the thatch area. Work with dark corn over eight squares from hole to hole. The colour pattern is two stitches of dark corn then one of light corn, repeated along the row. Take the line up over the window, as shown in the chart, keeping the stitch length correct. Start the second row six squares up from the first. The long stitches overlap the first row with two squares. Start with one stitch of light corn, then two of dark corn, again repeating this along the row. The third row is as the first row. In the fourth row the stitches are 10 squares in length. Overlap in the same way and begin with light corn, then dark corn. The fifth row is again 10 squares high, and starts with two stitches of dark corn and then one of light corn. The final row is 13 squares high. Work one stitch of light corn, and then two of dark corn.

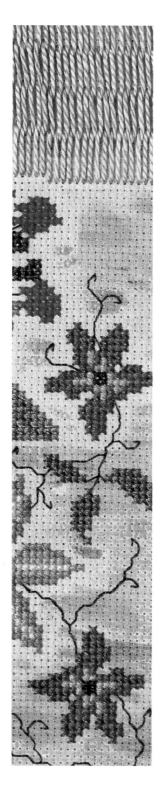

CHART KEY • Cat and Clematis

Symbol	Colour	Thread	Stitch
A	Dark grey	DMC stranded cotton: 535 (2 str)	Simple cross stitch
1	Dark purple maroon	DMC stranded cotton: 3802 (2 str)	Simple cross stitch
2	Terracotta	DMC stranded cotton: 920 (2 str)	Simple cross stitch
5	Light purple	DMC stranded cotton: 211 (2 str)	Simple cross stitch
V	White	DMC stranded cotton: blanc (2 str)	Simple cross stitch
C	Dark red	DMC stranded cotton: 815 (2 str)	Simple cross stitch
◁	Purple	DMC stranded cotton: 209 (2 str)	Simple cross stitch
E	Rich dark green	DMC stranded cotton: 3345 (2 str)	Simple cross stitch
▬	Maroon	DMC stranded cotton: 3803 (2 str)	Simple cross stitch
▲	Bright red	DMC stranded cotton: 498 (2 str)	Simple cross stitch
↑	Dark purple	DMC stranded cotton: 553 (2 str)	Simple cross stitch
●	Blue green	DMC stranded cotton: 368 (2 str)	Simple cross stitch
K	Dark green	DMC stranded cotton: 3051 (2 str)	Simple cross stitch
⊓	Pale pink	DMC stranded cotton: 3713 (2 str)	Simple cross stitch
N	Pale yellow Light sand	DMC stranded cotton: 745 (1 str) DMC stranded cotton: 738 (1 str)	Simple cross stitch
P	Dark terracotta	DMC stranded cotton: 918 (2 str)	Simple cross stitch
＼	Dull brown	DMC stranded cotton: 610 (2 str)	Simple cross stitch
Ⅰ	Darkest grey	DMC stranded cotton: 3799 (2 str)	Simple cross stitch
⊘	Golden sand	DMC stranded cotton: 436 (2 str)	Simple cross stitch
W	Light dull brown	DMC stranded cotton: 611 (2 str)	Simple cross stitch
X	Darkest purple	DMC stranded cotton: 208 (2 str)	Simple cross stitch
3	Black	DMC stranded cotton: 310 (2 str)	Simple cross stitch
	Dark corn	DMC Perle No 5: 612 (1 str)	Long straight stitch
	Light corn	DMC Perle No 5: 613 (1 str)	Long straight stitch
	White	DMC stranded cotton: Blanc (1 str)	Long straight stitch
	Blue shades	DMC stranded cotton: 124 (3 str)	Long diagonal stitch
	Very dark green	DMC stranded cotton: 934 (1 str)	Backstitch
	Stone	DMC stranded cotton: 3032 (1 str)	Backstitch
	Black	DMC stranded cotton: 310 (1 str)	Backstitch
	White	DMC stranded cotton: Blanc (1 str)	Backstitch

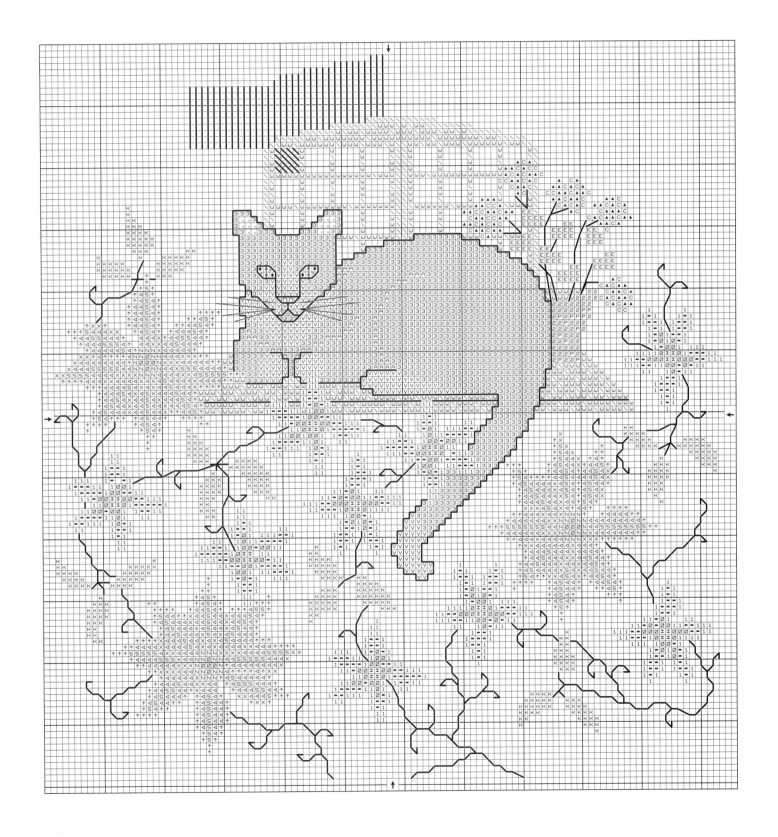

121

Basic Skills

PREPARING THE FABRIC

Even with an average amount of handling, many evenweave fabrics tend to fray at the edges. It is advisable to overcast the raw edges with ordinary sewing thread before you begin.

THE INSTRUCTIONS

Each project includes a full list of materials you will require. The fabrics are all produced by Zweigart, and a brief description of each fabric is given in the What You Will Need section (see page 8) if you want to find an alternative. The size given includes an allowance on all sides of approximately 6 cm (2⅜ in) for a large project. If you are unsure how much allowance is given for each project, the design size is given at the beginning of each project for information.

The colour keys are given for all threads used in each project, and clearly displayed in a highlighted box. I have not used more than one skein for any one design. If you want to work the project in a different make of thread ask your supplier, or your local needlework centre, for a conversion chart.

You may prefer to have some of the detailed charts enlarged to make working easier. I often use a photocopy which I mark with a pencil when I have completed an area of stitching; this makes colour recognition easier. A photocopying service will usually make enlargements for a minimal fee.

Before you begin to embroider, always mark the centre of the design with two lines of basting stitches, one vertical and one horizontal, running from edge to edge of the fabric, as indicated by the arrows on the charts. As you stitch, use the centre lines given on the chart and the basting threads on your fabric as reference points for counting the squares and threads to position your design accurately

BASIC STITCHES

Simple Cross Stitch

For all simple cross stitch embroidery, the following two methods of working are used. In each case, neat rows of vertical stitches are produced on the back of the fabric.

When stitching large areas of one colour, work in horizontal rows. Working from left to right, bring the needle up in the bottom left square and take it down in the top right square, making a diagonal stitch. Complete the first row of evenly spaced diagonal stitches over the number of threads specified in the project instructions. Then, working from right to left, repeat the process, bringing the needle up in the bottom right square and taking it down in the top left square. Continue in this way, making sure that each stitch crosses in the same direction.

When stitching diagonal lines of simple cross stitch, work downwards, completing each stitch before moving to the next. When starting a project, always begin to embroider at the centre of the design and work outwards to ensure that the design is placed centrally on the fabric.

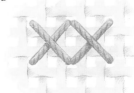

Simple cross stitch

Backstitch

Backstitch is used to give emphasis to a particular foldline, an outline or a shadow. The stitches are worked over the same number of threads as the simple cross stitch, forming continuous straight or diagonal lines.

Make the first stitch from left to right; pass the needle behind the fabric and bring it out one stitch length ahead to the left. Repeat and continue in this way along the line.

Backstitch

SYMBOLS

Some symbols used on the charts depict two different threads used in one needle; this is shown clearly on the colour key. Symbols to depict long cross stitch may be found on a chart; this is explained in the text, and is clear on the colour key.

WORKING IN A HOOP

A wooden hoop consists of two circles, one fitting inside the other, and the outer one having a screw at the top for tightening the hoops together. The fabric is placed between the two pieces and gently stretched as the screw is tightened until gradually the fabric is made tight, and when you tap it with your knuckles it sounds like a drum. As you tighten the fabric make sure the grain is straight.

Working in a hoop

BINDING A HOOP

Before using the hoop for the first time it is a good idea to bind the inner ring with bias binding, which prevents the fabric being marked. Once the hoop is bound it can be used time and time again.

Begin at the top edge of the inner ring and secure the bias binding using a few small stitches. Wind the binding around the hoop, overlapping it slightly so that the binding makes a continuous line around the wood. Finish at the top edge as before.

DRESSING A SLATE FRAME

It is well worth spending some time on this if you are about to work a complicated or sizeable project. If you are working either the goldwork project or the beading project, it is a good idea to dress the frame fully.

The fabric is prepared by overcasting the edges to prevent it fraying. The sides of the larger pieces of fabric need to be reinforced in the following way. Turn a 2.5 cm (½ in) hem and machine in

place. Take a piece of cord or string and thread down the hem on each side, then stitch in place at the upper and lower edges.

The fabric is now ready to be attached to the frame. Begin at the centre of the upper edge of fabric, and the centre of the top roller bar (making sure the loose edge of tape is facing inwards). Hem stitch the fabric to the tape edge from the centre to the right-hand edge, and then from the centre to the left-hand edge.

Turn the frame around and complete the other roller bar in the same way. Tighten the fabric by turning the roller bars around, winding the fabric round.

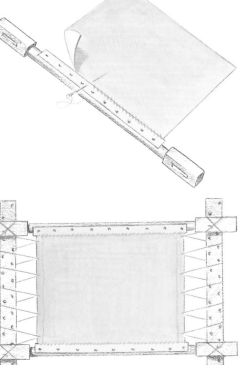

Dressing a slate frame

When the centre of the fabric is in the centre of the frame tighten the wing nuts to secure the fabric.

Lace the sides as follows. Thread a large needle with a thick strong thread (Perle No 5 is excellent). Start with a knot at the top left-hand edge and take the thread around the wooden side bar and back through the edge of the fabric (embracing the strengthened edge). Repeat this all the way along the side, and make stitches about 2.5 cm (1 in) apart. When you reach the lower edge, tighten the lacing before securing. Repeat for the second side.

When you have worked the area visible and need to move the fabric in the frame, cut the lacing threads, and wind the roller bars to select another area, then lace again.

The frame is now dressed and ready. Here is one further piece of advice: if you turn the frame over so that the wing nuts at the corners are facing you and work from this side, you should not mark the fabric on the roller bars.

FRAME COVERS

I am a bit of a fuss-pot about covering my work when it is not in use. I usually make a small bag to slide the hoops into when I put work down at the end of the day. The bag can be secured with drawstrings at the open end, and these are drawn up enough to enclose the work but not too tightly or fabric can be creased. A large slate frame will usually fit into an old pillowcase, and a floor-standing frame will benefit from being covered by a cloth. Plain white cotton or calico is best, but any clean colourfast fabric will do.

WASHING INSTRUCTIONS

If your completed cross stitch embroidery looks a bit grubby, you can wash it carefully. However, beware of goldwork threads as these are not meant to be washed. Most goldwork is carried out on coloured fabric, and is less likely to look shabby.

Wash your work as follows. Immerse the work into hand-hot water with a gentle cleanser, but not a detergent. Agitate it gently and leave to soak rather than scrub at problem areas. Rinse and place face-down on a clean colourfast terry towel. Leave until almost dry, then press on the back gently with a warm iron until completely dry. Do not use too hot an iron if you are in any doubt about the items stitched on to the right side of the fabric, and keep the iron moving constantly.

MOUNTING EMBROIDERY

The cardboard should be cut to the size of the finished embroidery, with an extra 6 mm (¼ in) added all around to allow for the recess in the frame.

Lightweight fabrics

1 Place the embroidery face down, with the cardboard centred on top, and basting and pencil lines matching. Begin by folding over the fabric at each corner and securing it with masking tape.
2 Working first on one side and then the other, fold over the fabric on all sides and secure it firmly with pieces of masking tape, placed about 2.5 cm (1 in) apart. Neaten the mitred corners with masking tape, pulling the fabric tightly to give a firm, smooth finish.

Heavier fabrics

Lay the emboidery face down, with the cardboard centred on top; fold over the edges of the fabric on opposite sides, making mitred folds at the corners, and lace across, using strong thread. Repeat on the other two sides. Finally, pull up the fabric firmly over the cardboard. Overstitch the mitred corners.

Conversion Chart

The threads listed in the first column of each conversion table are the threads actually used for that project.
You may find that if you use threads from another thread company the shades will vary slightly. These conversion tables
are for stranded cottons and Perle 5 threads only. Refer to the actual project for details of other threads used.

Stargazer Lily Brooch

ANCHOR	DMC
25	776
26	894
268	580
295	726
308	781

Foxglove Panel

DMC	ANCHOR
310	403
319	217
340	118
501	878
502	877
726	295
744	301
745	300
890	218
986	246
987	258
988	257
989	56
3045	943
3053	860
3350	78
3354	75
3685	69
3687	68
3688	66
3713	1020

Church Window

ANCHOR	DMC
392	642
903	3032

Kingfisher Panel

ANCHOR	DMC
white	white
152	939
164	824
168	597
169	806
170	517
268	580
273	3787
349	301
368	436
369	434
370	400
403	310
854	3012
858	646
859	3053
860	3052
861	3052
877	502
879	500
898	612

Christmas Tree

ANCHOR	DMC
212	991
923	699

Herb Garden Cushion

ANCHOR	DMC
white	white
23	819
25	776
96	554
98	553
109	210
128	800
210	562
261	368
262	3363
263	3362
265	471
266	470
267	469
292	3078
295	726
357	433
372	738
373	739

Oak Leaf Bookmark

DMC	ANCHOR
469	267
470	266
780	309
782	307
936	846

Pin Cushion

ANCHOR	DMC
90	554

Elephant Cushion

DMC	ANCHOR
white	white
646	8581
648	900
729	890
902	72
934	862
964	185
3042	870

Winter Window

ANCHOR	DMC
262	3363
859	3053
969	316

Conversion Chart

continued

Delphiniums Picture

ANCHOR	DMC
90	554
108	211
117	341
212	561
263	3362
268	580
862	934
871	3041
878	501

Garden Gate

ANCHOR	DMC
75	604
76	603
78	601
108	211
128	800
210	562
212	991
261	368
262	3363
265	471
265	471
266	470
268	580
293	640
349	301
368	436
369	434
403	310
877	502
878	501
1030	3746

Waterfall

ANCHOR	DMC
white	white
232	452
235	318
265	471
266	470
268	580
380	839
920	932

Lily Pond

ANCHOR	DMC
white	white
73	3689
75	602
76	603
78	601
117	341
118	340
208	913
242	913
244	702
258	904
261	368
264	472
265	471
267	469
292	3078
293	727
295	726
339	920
358	433

ANCHOR	DMC
372	738
373	739
400	645
403	310
843	3013
875	504
876	503
877	502
878	501
885	677
898	612
926	712

Butterfly Picture

ANCHOR	DMC
118	340
119	333
293	727
339	414
357	433
372	738
374	437
381	838
403	310
944	869

Goldwork Sampler

ANCHOR	DMC
164	824
168	807
169	906

Tulip Tray Cloth

ANCHOR	DMC
1207	116
1216	94

Cat and Clematis

DMC	ANCHOR
white	white
124	1210
208	111
209	110
211	108
310	403
368	214
436	363
498	47
535	401
553	98
610	905
611	889
612	898
613	853
738	361
745	300
815	22
918	341
920	339
934	862
3032	392
3051	862
3345	268
3713	1020
3799	236
3802	1019
3803	972

General Suppliers

Threads: UK

COATS PATONS CRAFTS UK
Customer Services
McMullen Road, Darlington
Co Durham DL1 1YO

DMC CREATIVE WORLD LTD
Pullman Road, Wigston
Leicestershire LE18 2DY

MADIERA THREADS UK LTD
Thirsk Industrial Park
York Road, Thirsk
North Yorkshire YO7 3BX

Threads: USA

COATS & CLARK
PO Box 27067, Dept CO1
Greenville SC 29616

THE DMC CORPORATION
Port Kearney Building
10 South Kearney
NJ 07032-0650

MADEIRA MARKETING LTD
600 East 9th Street, Michigan City
IN 46360

Threads: AUSTRALIA

COATS PATONS CRAFTS
Thistle Street, Launceston
Tasmania 7250

DMC NEEDLECRAFT PTY
PO Box 317, Earlswood 2206
NSW 2204

PENGUIN THREADS PTY LTD
25-27 Izett Street, Prahran
Victoria 3181

Brooch: *page 13*
Reference no 10
ELIZABETH ANDERSON MINIATURES
Rosedale, Tall Elms Close, Bromley
Kent BR2 0TT

Cards: *pages 24, 32 and 65*
Page 24: Type T small church window
Size 118 mm x 91 mm (14⅜ in x 3 in),
aperture 81 mm x 55 mm (3⅛ in x 2 in)
gold; Reference no 1423
Page 32: White card in the shape of a
Christmas tree
Size 114 mm x 89 mm (4½ in x 3½ in),
aperture 80 mm x 64 mm (3¼ in x 2½ in)
Page 65: Type T church window
Size 154 mm x 111 mm (6 in x 4 in), arch
aperture 111 mm x 71 mm (4 in x 2¾ in)

IMPRESS CARDS AND CRAFT MATERIALS
Slough Farm, Westhall, Halesworth
Suffolk IP19 8RN

Beads: *pages 55-59, 67 and 104*
SPOILT FOR CHOICE
35 March Road, Wimblington, March
Cambridgeshire PE15 0RW

CREATIVE BEADCRAFT LTD
Denmark Works
Sheepcote Dell Road, Beamond End
nr Amersham
Buckinghamshire HP7 0RX

Sequins and beads: *page 55*
Sequins 6mm flat gunmetal, reference
1326
Bugle bead gold reference 1402
3mm gold bead reference 1521
Beading straws reference 1721

NEVILLES TEXTILES
PO Box 87, 29 Stoney Street
Nottingham NT1 1LR

Cushion: *page 59*
Cushion finishing kit, windsor blue

RUSSELL HOUSE TAPESTRIES
13 Church Street, Wiveliscombe
Somerset TA4 2LR

Stitch magnet: *page 56*
HUMMINGBIRD HOUSE
PO Box 2, Lochearnhead, Perthshire
Scotland FK19 8PL

Ribbons: *page 64*
Small silk ribbons 2mm (⅛in) thick

RIBBON DESIGNS
4 Lake View, Edgware
Middlesex HA8 7RU

**Frame for landscape and butterfly
picture**: *pages 77 and 101*
Alec George
KERNOCRAFT
Wheal Virgin House, Unit 5 Consols
St Ives, Cornwall TR26 2HW

Stencil stockists: *page 112*
P & O DIANE HUCK
Oak Tree Cottages, Evesbatch
Bishops Frome
Worcestershire WR6 5BE

STENCIL EASE
LEISURE PRODUCTS UK LTD
PO Box 3, Cleobury Mortimer
Shropshire DY14 8BJ

Transparent fabrics: *page 92*
BITS & PIECES
4 Thorold Road, Bitterne Park
Southampton SO18 1JB

Index

Aida blockweave, 10

backstitch, 122
beading, 55-63
beading straws, 00
beads, 9
binding hoops, 123
blending filaments, 0
blending threads, 8, 22-9
blockweave, Aida, 10
bookmark, oak leaf, 41-3
Brooch, Stargazer Lily, 13-14
Butterfly Picture, 101-3

Cat and Clematis, 116-21
chain stitch, detached, 85
chart holders, 0
Christmas Tree, 32-3
Church Window, 24-5
cotton threads, 8
couching, 0
crewel wools, 8
cushions:
    Elephant Cushion, 59-63
    Herb Garden Cushion, 34-9
    Pincushion, 57-8

daylight bulbs, 10
Delphiniums Picture, 67-75
detached chain stitch, 85
double cross stitch, 30-31
dyeing, 112, 116-21

Elephant Cushion, 59-63
evenweave fabrics, 10
eyelet stitch, 47

fabrics, 10
flower threads, 8
fly stitch, 107
Foxglove Panel, 15-21
frame covers, 123
frames, 11
    slate frames, 11,123
french knots, 78

garden gate, 80-88
goldwork, 100-111
graph paper, 11

half cross stitch, 0
half stitch, 0
Herb Garden Cushion, 34-9
hoops, 10-11, 122-3

Kingfisher Panel, 26-9
knots, 76-88
    french knots, 78
    lark's head knots, 0
Kreinik threads, see blending
    filaments

lark's head knots, 0
light bulbs, 10
lily pond, 92-9
long cross stitch, 23
loops, 76
    beaded, 56

magnets, 11
magnifying equipment, 10
Marlitt threads, see rayon
    threads

materials, 8-10
metallic threads, 8
mounting embroidery, 124
needles, 11
    beading straws, 0

oak leaf bookmark, 41-3

painting fabric, 112-15
patterns, stitching, 40-54
perlé cotton, 8
Pincushion, 57-8

rayon threads, 8
ribbons, 8, 64-75
rice stitch, 47

Sampler, 104-11
scissors, 11
seams, beaded, 56
seat frames, 11
semi-sheer fabrics, 10, 89-99
simple cross stitch, 12-21, 122
slate frames, 11, 123
Small Landscape, 77-9
Stargazer Lily Brooch, 13-14
stencilling fabric, 0
stitches, 122-3
    backstitch, 122
    detached chain stitch, 85
    double cross stitch, 30-31
    eyelet stitch, 47
    fly stitch, 107
    french knots, 78
    half cross stitch, 0
    half stitch, 0

long cross stitch, 23
rice stitch, 47
simple cross stitch, 12, 122
straight stitch, 0
tent stitch, 0
wheatsheaf stitch, 0
straight stitch, 0
stranded cotton, 8
symbols, 122

tassels, beaded, 56
tent stitch, 0
thread organizers, 0
threads, 8
    blending, 22-3
tools, 10-11
tracing graph paper, 11
Tray Cloth, Tulip, 113-15
trolley needles, 11
Tudor House, 44-54
Tulip Tray Cloth, 113-15

washing instructions, 124
waterfall, 90-91
wheatsheaf stitch, 0
Winter Window, 65-6
wools, 8

ACKNOWLEDGEMENTS

The publishers wish to express their thanks to the following people and organisations for their very expedient help:

For the loan of threads and ribbons for photography on the cover and page 9: Julie Gill, COATS PATONS CRAFTS (address on page 127)

For the loan of beads for photography on the cover and page 9: Tracy Ells, CREATIVE BEADCRAFT LTD (address on page 127)

For the loan of transparent fabric for photography on page 9: BITS & PIECES (address on page 127)